VOGUE

CHRISTMAS

VOGUE

CHRISTMAS

HARPER & ROW, PUBLISHERS, NEW YORK
Cambridge, Philadelphia, San Francisco, London, Mexico City,
São Paulo, Sydney

Writer: Marion Bartholomew

Illustrator: Phoebe Adams Gaughan

Editor: Helen Moore

Coordinator for Butterick: Patricia Perry

Butterick staff: Jane Glanzer, Carol Sharma, Shirley Asper, Barbara Geibar, Renee Ullman

Coordinator for Harper & Row: Carol Cohen

Harper & Row production staff: Mary Chadwick, Lydia Link, Coral Tysliava

FIRST EDITION

Designed by Betty Binns Graphics

Library of Congress Cataloging in Publication Data
Main entry under title:

Vogue Christmas.

Includes index.
1. Christmas decorations.   2. Textile crafts.
3. Sewing.
TT900.C4V64 1984   746.9   84-47560
ISBN 0-06-181126-2

84 85 86 87 88 10 9 8 7 6 5 4 3 2 1

Contents

How to use this book, 7

Craft Techniques

Decorating the Tree

Decorating Your Home

Gifts and Gift Wrapping

COLOR INSERT FOLLOWS PAGE 48.

How to use this book

Vogue Christmas is divided into two sections. First you'll find a listing of craft techniques with explanations of, and instructions for, the variety of different techniques necessary to create all the fabulous projects offered in *Vogue Christmas*. These craft techniques, beginning on p. 10, have been arranged alphabetically with many helpful cross references to make this book easy to use. This format was specifically chosen to help you make any of these beautiful Christmas projects, but also to help you when you sew crafts throughout the years.

The majority of *Vogue Christmas* is devoted to projects. *Vogue Christmas* contains many beautiful and useful items to make for the holiday season. Decorate your tree with delicately embroidered ornaments, an heirloom treetop angel, and a regal tree skirt. Decorate your home with the old world charm of a nosegay wreath, the jolly smiling Santa Christmas card holder, and an assortment of table decorations that sing out the spirit of the season. And what best conveys the spirit of Christmas than lovingly handmade gifts? *Vogue Christmas* lets you select from an assortment of gifts for all the special people in your life. Choose either the sleeping baby or the teddy bear for your favorite preschooler. Give your favorite businessperson a monogrammed briefcase to carry important papers. Pamper your friends by giving a collection of padded hangers and sachets. You'll find other enticing projects beginning on p. 50. Each project includes a listing of materials needed as well as complete how-to instructions.

PATTERNS

Whenever possible, full size patterns have been provided, beginning on p. 143. To use, simply trace them onto tracing paper to make your pattern pieces and then cut them from your fabric. Pattern pieces too large to fit on the book page have been reduced to one-half or one-quarter of their actual size to make enlarging as easy as possible. You'll find complete instructions for enlarging on p. 29.

For some projects, no pattern pieces are necessary, all that is required is the cutting of squares or rectangles, and the dimensions for these are provided with the how-to instructions. For some of these, a curved corner or end is called for, and a corner guide for cutting the proper curves is given.

The pattern pieces included in this book do not have seamlines marked on them. The heavy solid lines given are cutting lines. All seam allowances are built into the pattern, the seam allowance width for each project appears in the How-To section.

CUTTING

No cutting layouts are given. You will find the number of pieces to cut and the material to use listed in every project. When necessary, the pattern pieces have grainlines that are to be placed on the lengthwise or crosswise grain of the fabric. Other pieces have this symbol, ┌─────┐, which indicates that the arrow is to be placed on the fold of the fabric; when cutting, do *not* cut along this fold. Pattern pieces with no grainlines can be cut to utilize the fabric the best way. Notches can be cut with the point out or marked another way (see below). When "Cut 2" is listed for a piece, use a double layer of fabric and cut the pattern piece once, or use a single layer of fabric and cut it twice. When using a single layer, be sure to cut one piece with the pattern facing up and one piece with the pattern facing down. When "Cut 1" is listed, lay the pattern piece right side up on the right side of a single layer of fabric. If you are using fabrics that have nap, shading, or a one-way design, cut all the pieces in the same direction. These fabrics, to give you some examples, are corduroy, velvet, satin, eyelet, fake fur, lace, sequinned types, synthetic suedes, and taffeta.

MARKING

Before you remove the pattern piece from your fabric, mark all symbols, notches (if you did not cut them with the point out), placement lines and foldlines. Always mark on the *wrong* side of your fabric. Use dressmaker's tracing paper and a tracing wheel, dressmaker's chalk pencil, or a soft lead pencil. In some cases you may have pieces where the fabric is identical on both sides and there are no pattern markings to tell you which side is to be used as the right side. When this happens, mark the wrong side of the fabric with masking tape or a soft lead pencil or chalk, in the seam allowance. If the pieces are not easily identifiable, write each piece name on the masking tape or in the seam allowance.

Craft Techniques

Adhesives

When your project instructions call for pieces to be glued or bonded together, you'll get the best results if you choose the adhesive that is the most suitable for the materials you are using. If you are going to wash or dry clean your project, make sure you are using a glue that is permanent *and* not affected by washing. Fusible web, for example, is an adhesive that is both permanent, washable, and dry cleanable. Check adhesive labels and/or test washability on scraps of fabric or trim first. Temporary glues (some glue sticks and sprays for instance) should not be used if your project will be washed or dry cleaned. The 3 basic types of adhesives are glue, double-faced tape, and fusible web.

GLUES

White glue

White craft glue, such as Elmer's and Sobo, creates a strong bond and dries clear, but it must be spread evenly to avoid hard lumps when it is dry. It is a good all-purpose permanent glue for medium to heavy weight fabrics. Test it first on some scraps of your fabric or trim to make sure it doesn't soak through and stain the right side. White glue can be easily washed off with water *before* it dries.

Tacky white glue

This type (Aleene's is one brand) works as well as regular white glue but generally will not soak into fabrics. It is a permanent glue recommended for use on felt, ribbons, and other lightweight, loosely woven, or non-woven fabrics and trims.

Glue stick

An excellent adhesive for applying trims that will be stitched down and for spot gluing when only a temporary adhesive is needed. Make sure the stick you buy is appropriate for fabrics.

Spray adhesive

Although it saves time, this adhesive can be hard to manage. You must work in an area with proper ventilation. A spray adhesive works well with light to medium weight fabrics since its tackiness allows repositioning, but it's only good when a temporary adhesive is needed. Remember to read and follow all package instructions.

Electric hot glue gun

This craft tool looks like a soldering gun; many crafters consider it an invaluable aid when working on no-sew and non-fabric projects. It is excellent for spot gluing and for applying glue to difficult-to-reach areas.

DOUBLE-FACED TAPES

Basting tape

Available in a ⅛" (3mm) width, basting tape makes it easy to attach straight rows of lightweight, narrow trims such as ribbon, wide rickrack, and thin braid. It can also be used for holding small pieces of fabric together for stitching. Position the tape so you will not stitch into it, as the adhesive will gum up your machine needle, affecting the stitch formation.

Other double-faced tapes can be used when you need an instant bond and glue would be messy or inappropriate—such as for holding fabric in place on the back of mat board as it is being stretched and smoothed over the front for a picture frame. For the strongest hold,

PERMANENT ADHESIVE AND MATERIALS GUIDE

Materials	white glue	tacky white glue	fusible web
fabric to fabric or batting	x	x	x
fabric to mat board	x	x	x
felt		x	x
batting to batting	x	x	
batting to mat board	x	x	
mat board to mat board	x	x	
fabric trims to fabric	x	x	x
non-fabric trims to fabric	x	x	
synthetic leathers and suedes	x	x	x

look for double-faced *carpet* tape. *Double-stick* tape is transparent and comes in a dispenser, but is good only for light-duty work. If you are going to use any double-faced tape in conjunction with glue, test first to see if the glue will in any way come in contact with the tape, either directly or as a result of soaking through another material. The moisture of the glue could cause the tape to lose its adhesive ability.

FUSIBLE WEB

For bonding fabric to fabric, or batting and flat trims to fabric, fusible web is a real time-saver. The web can be cut into any shape, comes by the yard or as a tape, is invisible after heat and steam are applied, and is permanent, washable, and dry cleanable. Always test the fusible web to make sure it is compatible with the fabric and/or trims you will be using. Carefully follow the manufacturer's directions for fusing. Avoid fabrics and trims that will be affected by heat and steam. Keep in mind that fusible web should be used only on smooth, flat-surfaced fabrics and trims, as the use of the steam iron could flatten pile and surface textures.

Appliqué

An appliqué is a shaped piece of fabric that is attached to the surface of a larger piece of fabric, to create a raised effect. It can be sewn on by machine with either zigzag or straight stitching, sewn by hand, or fused in place.

BY MACHINE

This method of appliqué requires no seam allowances. Cut the appliqué shapes to their exact finished size, on the seamline. (All appliqué patterns in this book are given without seam allowances.) For each appliqué shape, cut a piece of fusible web the same size or slightly smaller (see Adhesives, p. 10). The fusible web will securely anchor your appliqué until you stitch it in place. Hand or pin-basted appliqués can shift position while you are stitching them.

If your appliqué design has several different and overlapped shapes, begin with the undermost piece. Position the appliqué, right side up on the background fabric, following pattern placement lines or your own design. Sandwich the fusible web between the appliqué and the background fabric (A).

Fuse in place, following manufacturer's directions for the fusible web.

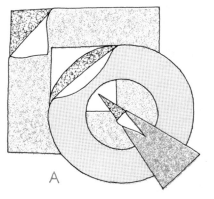

Stitching

With the appliqué securely fused in place, machine zigzag the edges of the appliqué. Use a narrow to medium width zigzag stitch and a very short stitch length to produce a smooth, even, satinlike stitch. Generally, the smaller the appliqué and the more curves, the narrower your stitch width should be. Always test first on some fabric scraps to make sure you are satisfied with the stitch settings. Begin stitching with the appliqué to the left of the needle whenever possible. The right swing of the needle should go into the background fabric just beside the edge of the appliqué (B). Stitch slowly around all the edges in this manner. Hold the needle thread to the back of the needle as you take the first few stitches. When your stitching meets, finish the stitching as close as you can to the beginning stitches. Remove the project from the machine. Pull your threads to the wrong side, tie them together, and trim them.

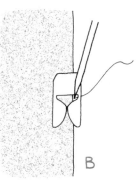

Corners

For outside corners, stitch to the end of the fabric. Stop with the needle in the right-hand position, but still aligned with the appliqué. Pivot the fabric and continue along the next edge (C).

For inside corners, stitch past the corner, onto the appliqué, for just the width of the zigzag stitch, stopping with the needle in the left-hand position. Pivot the fabric and continue stitching (D).

Curves

On outside curves, pivot the fabric slightly to accommodate the curve when the needle is in its right-hand position. Stitch slowly, pivoting the fabric whenever the needle goes too far off the edge of the appliqué curve (E).

Inside curves are pivoted when the needle is in its left-hand position. Stitching slowly, pivot whenever the needle goes too far in from the edge of the curve (F).

Points

Stitch until the left-hand position of the needle is just off the left edge. Pivot the fabric slightly so the point is centered under the presser foot, decrease the stitch width so the stitching goes across the point and just into the background fabric on both sides. As you slowly stitch, continue decreasing the stitch width until it is at or near zero, to form the point. Pivot, and begin increasing the stitch width until you reach the original stitch width (G).

For the best control of your stitching, hold the fabric taut with your left hand behind the needle, gently guiding it as needed. Use your right hand to guide the appliqué under the needle.

For felt appliqués, you can use a straight machine stitch close to the appliqué edge instead of zigzag, if desired.

BY HAND

How you sew the appliqué depends on the type of fabric you are using. For felt, you need no seam allowances, but for all other fabrics add a ¼″ (6mm) seam allowance all around each appliqué piece.

After each appliqué piece is cut, stitch just inside the seamline all around. Clip the fabric to the stitching line (H).

Rolling the stitches to the wrong side, press the seam allowances, carefully shaping any curves. Baste (I).

Position the appliqué on the background fabric, according to

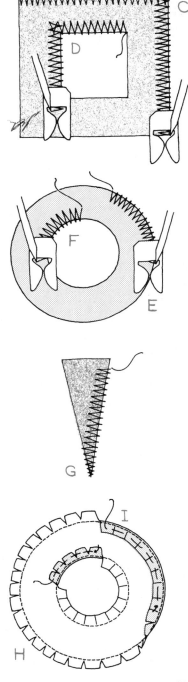

your pattern, or your own design. Pin, baste, or fuse in place. For woven fabrics, when an invisible stitch is desired, slipstitch (see Hand Sewing, p. 34) in place with matching thread. For either woven fabric or felt, when a decorative stitch is desired, sew in place using a blanket stitch (see Embroidery, p. 25). Remove basting.

NON-STITCHED APPLIQUÉS

For a quick way to attach appliqués cut from felt or a tightly woven fabric that does not ravel, consider fusing them in place. Another option is to glue them in place (see Adhesives, p. 10). Test first on scraps of fabric.

Backstitch

See **Hand Sewing,** *and* **Machine Stitching**

Batting

Used to add thickness, soft-ness, and body to craft proj-ects, batting is available as a sheet of fluffy material that you can cut to size for your project. Most battings are made of polyester and/or cotton fibers.

Batting comes in different thicknesses, called lofts, a fac-tor to consider, depending on your project's size and use. For small items such as tree orna-ments, a thinner, less lofty batt is appropriate. For a larger project, such as a tree skirt, a thicker batt with more bulk and more body is a good choice. If you want the thickness but can find only thin batts, use several layers of the thin batt to get the loft that you desire.

Batting is sold by the yard or in prepackaged sizes that coor-dinate to quilt measurements. Since most craft projects use only small amounts of batting, the crib-quilt-size package should provide what you need. Check your project require-ments to be sure.

Polyester fleece is a tighter, or denser, version of batting. It is not as soft as regular batting and has minimal thickness. It can be used instead of batting, and for small projects it may be easier to use because it is more stable than batting. It is sold by the yard, usually 40″ (101.5cm) wide, and will keep your costs down if you need only a small amount of batting. One or two layers of fleece is a good alter-native to batting in this case.

Probably the most important thing to know about handling batting and fleece is that they *must* be basted in place. For small projects that measure no more than 6″ (15cm) across, basting around the edges will do. For larger ones, add rows of basting across and up and down the batting in addition to around the edges. Batting not basted in place could shift in-side your project as you finish it, and create lumps.

Batting or fleece can be suc-cessfully hand sewn to itself, or to fabric. Do not sew batting alone on your machine. It is a material formed of many fibers, not woven from continuous threads like fabric, and the fi-bers could jam your machine.

Batting should always be sand-wiched between two fabric layers.

Many craft projects call for one or more layers of batting to be glued to something else. When gluing batting to another surface or to itself, spread the glue evenly on the surface the batting is to be glued to, or on the batting itself. Try to avoid leaving drops of glue. The drops will not flatten out when the batting is pressed over them, and they will create hard lumps that may show on the outside of your project.

Beads

Eye-catching and elegant beads, sequins, pearls, and paillettes are quite easy to apply. Beads and sequins work best with an outline to follow or fill in. If your project does not have a design for beading, the first step is to create your own design (see Transferring Designs, p. 47, for information on how to transfer beading designs to fabric).

TOOLS

For sewing beads or sequins to small areas of woven fabrics, you might find it helpful to use an embroidery hoop to hold the fabric taut. For felt and very firm fabrics, no hoop is needed. Large areas may need to be put into a quilting hoop or tacked to a stretcher frame (see Embroidery, p. 25).

Make sure that the area to be beaded lies fully within the hoop. Beads and sequins can break if they are placed between the two rings of an embroidery hoop, so if your design is just too large to fit any hoop, be careful to create an even tension with your stitches as you sew.

Look for the special long thin needles that are made to slip right through the beads and sequins with ease, for use on fine, sheer and light to medium weight fabrics. These beading needles are available at craft and fabric stores. Use a heavier needle for larger beads and heavy fabric or leather. Your thread must be strong, yet fine enough to go through the beads. Silk, nylon, and cotton-coated polyester threads are good choices. Add a coating of beeswax for more strength and to prevent the thread from tangling. For large and heavy beads, use button and carpet thread also coated with beeswax. Clear nylon thread is quite fine and does not show, but it tends to come unknotted at its ends (see Some Helpful Hints, p. 17).

SEWING BEADS

When beading in a random, or scattered design or when using very heavy beads, sew each one on with a backstitch (A). Small beads in rows can be sewn on several at a time. Pick up three or four on your needle—the number depends on how many you can string without the thread drooping in the middle of them. Take a

A

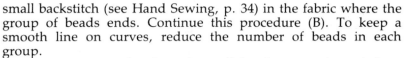

small backstitch (see Hand Sewing, p. 34) in the fabric where the group of beads ends. Continue this procedure (B). To keep a smooth line on curves, reduce the number of beads in each group.

Sew on prestrung beads with small hand overcasting stitches, sewing over the bead thread at intervals.

To create bead loops, bring the thread up from the wrong side of your fabric, string on the desired number of beads, then return the needle to the starting point (C). Knot the thread ends for each loop. Do not pull the threads too tightly, or the loops will become too stiff.

For a bead fringe, bring the needle up from the wrong side of your fabric, and string on the desired number of beads. At the end, string on one more bead, then bring the needle back up through the beads, using the bottom bead as a stopper (the thread will be seen on one side of this bottom bead). Bring the needle to the wrong side of the fabric, backstitch; then continue to the next strand of fringe. Do not pull the threads too tightly or the fringe will appear too rigid (D).

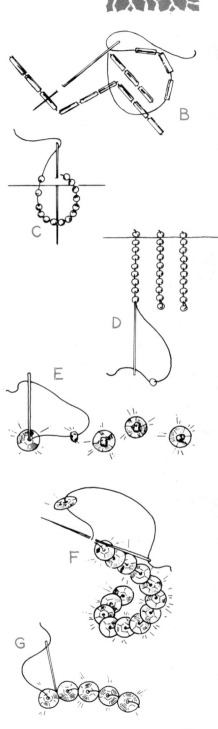

SEWING SEQUINS

These special sparklers can be sewn on individually in two different ways: with a bead or a single stitch.

For the bead application, bring the needle up through the sequin, pick up a bead, and insert the needle back down through the sequin. No thread will show on the sequin itself (E).

For the single stitch method, bring the needle up through the sequin. Insert the needle back into the fabric at the edge of the sequin. The thread will run across from the middle.

To sew sequins in rows, bring the needle up and string the sequins upside down. Take a backstitch from one edge of the sequin to the other, on the design line. As you pull up the thread, the sequin will flip over on its right side. Place the next sequin beside the first, upside down on the design line and repeat the stitch. The sequins will overlap and conceal the thread (F). You can also sew sequins in rows side by side, rather than overlapped, taking the thread across the sequins as when you are sewing them on individually (G).

Sew on paillettes (larger sequins, with holes near an edge) with a stitch from the hold to the edge or with a bead, as for sequins.

SOME HELPFUL HINTS

■ When sewing on large or heavy beads, or several beads at once, such as for a loop or fringe, use a doubled thread for extra strength.

- Keep the length of your thread short—no more than 10" (25cm)—to avoid tangling on its own and getting caught on beads and sequins already sewn in place.

- Keep your stitches even, and never tight, or your fabric will pucker.

- For extra security make frequent backstitches on the back of your fabric as you sew on the beads or sequins.

- Use a dot of clear nail polish on your thread knot to keep it tied.

- Avoid pressing beaded areas. Steam and heat from your iron could discolor or melt your beads and sequins. Press lightly around the beadwork if necessary, or lightly on the wrong side with a press cloth, with the work placed on a pressing pad or folded towel. Keep the iron off the beadwork.

Bias Binding

Literally, bias means a slant, and in terms of fabric and sewing, it is the diagonal grain of the fabric. Fabric strips cut on this bias grain can be folded and shaped to cover curved edges.

CUTTING YOUR OWN BIAS STRIPS

Individual bias strips

First, fold an end of your fabric diagonally to find the bias grain. The selvage of the folded edge should be at an exact right angle to the other selvage edge. This fold is the bias grain of your fabric. Crease or press the fold carefully to mark the bias grainline (A).

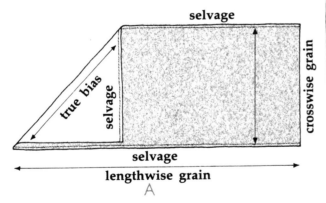

A

On the wrong side of the fabric and using the crease as a guide, mark strips the width you need. To determine the width, decide how wide the finished bias will be. Multiply this number by 4, and add an extra ⅛″–¼″ (3mm–6mm) for thin or tightly woven fabrics, or an extra ⅜″–½″ (10mm–13mm) for thick or

loosely woven fabrics, to allow for stretching and folding the bias. Mark enough strips until you have the length of bias you need for your project. Cut the strips apart, cutting the ends of the strips on the straight grain (B).

Join the ends, right sides together, in ¼″ (6mm) seams, matching the straight-grain ends. The strips will be at a right angle (C). Stitch, press open, then trim the triangular ends of the seam that extend beyond the sides of the strip (D).

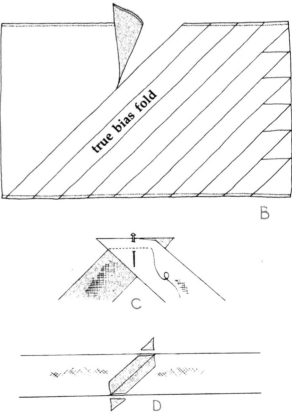

19

Continuous bias strips

When you need a long length of bias, save time by making one continuous length. Mark off a rectangle of fabric as for Individual Bias Strips, above, having all the strips the same length. Cut off the excess triangular ends on each side of the bias strip markings (E). With right sides together, form a tube so the short ends meet with one strip width extending at each end. Stitch the ends in a ¼″ (6mm) seam (F). Press the seam open. Cut the strips apart on the lines you marked, as shown (G).

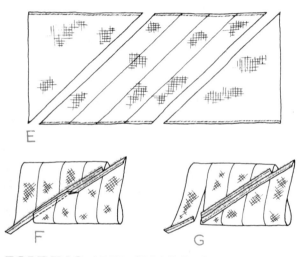

FOLDING AND SHAPING BIAS BINDING

Fold the binding in half, wrong sides together. Press lightly. Open the fold and turn in one raw edge to meet the center fold, and press. Turn in the remaining edge so it is slightly away from the fold, and press. Refold along the center and press again, stretching the bias evenly and gently to remove any slack (H).

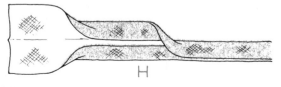

Before you sew the binding to any curved edge, shape it to match the curve, using a steam iron to set the curve.

SEWING BIAS BINDING

How you want your project to look can determine which application method you use. Attaching binding by hand is a two-step method that works for any project and is especially good for very curved as well as for small areas. Attaching binding by machine is a one-step method that works well for straight, slightly curved, or very long edges.

By hand

Preshape any curves, then open out the binding. With right sides together and raw edges even, pin the wider side of the binding to the right side of your project, allowing 2″ (5cm) for any overlapping ends. Begin and end the bias at the most inconspicuous place.

For overlapped ends, turn one end in ½″ (13mm) and lap it over the raw end. For an end that is at a finished edge, turn in the bias ½″ (13mm), matching the folded end of the bias with the finished edge of your project.

Stitch along the pressed fold of the bias nearest the raw edges (I). Fold the binding over to the wrong side of the fabric, encasing the raw edges, and pin. Slipstitch (see Hand Sewing, p. 34) the edge in place (J). Slipstitch any folded end(s) in place.

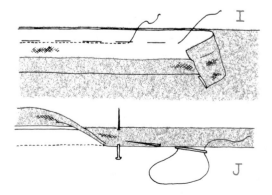

Inside corners

Reinforce the corner along the seamline, using small machine stitches. Clip the corner almost to the stitching (K). Pin the binding to the right side of your project. Stitch on the wrong side, opening out the corner so the raw edges are in a straight line, not at a right angle (L).

Press the binding up, forming a miter on the right side. Pull the miter through the clip to the wrong side, and form a miter in the opposite direction from the miter on the right side (M). Fold the bias over the raw edges, and slipstitch the binding and corner miters in place (N).

(O). Turn the binding to the wrong side, over the raw edges, forming another miter on the wrong side in the opposite direction from the miter on the right side. Slipstitch the binding and corners in place.

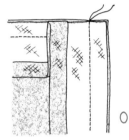

By machine

Preshape any curves. Then, with the narrower side of the binding on the right side of your project, encase the raw edge. Pin the binding in place. Cut any ends to be lapped on the straight grain. Turn in the overlapping end ½" (13mm) and lap this end over the raw end (P). For an end at a finished edge, turn under the raw end of the binding so the folded edge of the binding matches the finished edge of your project. On the right side, stitch close to the folded edge of the binding, catching in both edges of the bias. Stitch up and across the ends of the bias at a finished edge (Q). Slipstitch any overlapped edges if necessary.

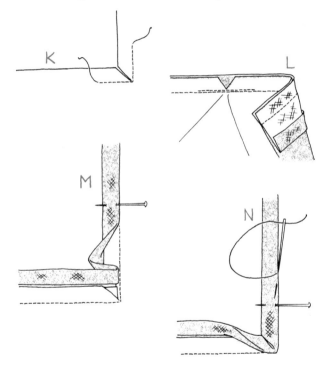

Outside corners

Stitch the binding to the point where the seam-lines on each side of the corner meet, back-stitching to secure (see Machine Stitching, p. 38). Remove your project from the machine. Turn the binding so the edges of the binding and fabric meet on the other side of the corner. Resume stitching, starting at the upper edge

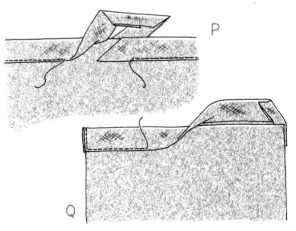

Inside corners

Reinforce and clip the corners as in K, above. Encase the edge with the binding, pinning it in place. Begin stitching, stopping at the inner point of the corner and keeping the needle in the fabric. Raise the presser foot and spread out the corner, straightening the edges. Continue to stitch on the binding. When you have finished, go back to the corners and fold the binding diagonally on the right side, pushing the binding fabric inside the binding. On the wrong side make a miter in the binding and press it flat (R). Machine stitch the miter, then slipstitch the corners in place.

Blanket Stitch

See **Embroidery**

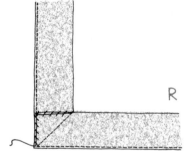

Outside corners

Sew on the binding to the edge of the corner. Turn the corner, forming a miter by folding the binding in diagonally at the corners on both sides. Resume stitching. Machine stitch the miter, then slipstitch the corner in place.

PURCHASED BIAS TAPE

Apply purchased double fold bias tape using either of the above methods.

Braid

FLAT BRAID

Many different types of flat braid trim are available: narrow, wide, fat, thin, glittery, and plain. Some can be sewn on, either by machine or by hand, while others can be successfully glued in place.

Sewing flat braid

Pin or baste the braid in place first. If the braid is ¼" (6mm) or wider, you can use double-faced basting tape for placement before you sew. Center the basting tape on the wrong side of the braid so there is enough room to stitch on either side. Sewing through the basting tape will gum up both hand and machine needles.

Very narrow braid can be sewn on with matching or contrasting thread using a zigzag stitch set at a medium to long stitch length. The zigzag will encase the braid.

If a wider braid surface is smooth and it fits easily under your machine's presser foot, sew the braid in place along both long edges, using matching thread. Turn under and lap the raw end you began with, if the ends are to meet (A). If the braid is to end at a finished edge, turn under the raw end of the braid at the edge. Always begin and end braid at the most inconspicuous place possible.

For braid that is too thick, sequinned, or otherwise unsuitable for machine stitching, sew both long edges in place by hand. If the braid ends are to meet, coat them with clear nail polish to keep them from fraying. Or, if the braid is firmly woven, you can whipstitch (see Hand Sewing, p. 34) the ends. Butt the ends together and sew them in place (B). Plan ahead so this joining occurs at the most inconspicuous place possible.

If the braid is loopy or loosely woven, wrap a piece of tape around both toes of your presser foot so the toes cannot catch the braid as you sew.

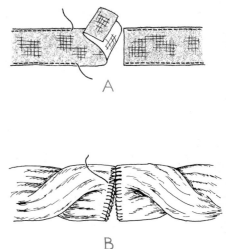

Gluing flat braid

Use glue to attach braid only if there are no seams to be sewn across the glued area. Test-glue a swatch of braid first to make sure the glue will not stain or seep through to the right side of your braid. Once the braid is glued, it's there to stay, so be sure to have all placement lines clearly marked on your project. After applying the braid, let the glue dry with the project lying flat, or, if the braid is near an edge, hold it in place with large paper clips, clothespins, or clamps.

On flat or thin braids, turn in and lap one end, gluing in place. For thick or other bulky braids, whipstitch the ends or coat them with clear nail polish and glue them, butted, in place.

FOLD-OVER BRAID

A decorative edge finish, fold-over braid is creased near the middle so it will fold over, or encase, an edge. It is very pliable and will take any shape, and is either braided or knitted. You can machine stitch it to an edge as you would bias binding (see p. 19). It is recommended that you hand baste the fold-over braid in place first; otherwise it has a tendency to shift. Fold-over braid can also be slipstitched in place, first on the right side, then on the wrong side of your project. For lapped ends, cut the ends straight. Pin one raw end in place, then turn under remaining end ½" (13mm) and lap.

Bullion Stitch
See **Embroidery**

Catchstitch
See **Hand Sewing**

Chain stitch
See **Embroidery**

Corners for Trims

Turning corners with trims (either flat braid, bands, laces, or ribbons) requires a simple miter. Stitch along inner edge of the trim to the lower edge. Fold back the trim on itself. Then turn the trim down so it turns the corner, making a diagonal fold across the corner. Press or crease this fold. Lift up the trim and stitch along the diagonal crease through all thicknesses (A). Continue in this manner, mitering and stitching all the corners. Finish by stitching the outer edge, pivoting at the corners.

If there is only one edge to be stitched down, as for some laces, form the corner miter the same way.

Couching Stitch
See **Embroidery**

Cross stitch
See **Embroidery**

Cut-Edge Ribbon
See **Ribbons**

Edgestitch
See **Machine Stitching**

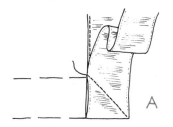

A

Embroidery

STITCHES

Blanket stitch

Secure your thread at the edge. Working from left to right and with the edge facing you, take the needle down to the wrong side anywhere from 3⁄16″ (5mm) to 1⁄2″ (13mm) above the edge. Keep the thread below the needle, draw the needle through the loop formed and pull the thread taut. Space the stitches evenly, from 3⁄16″ (5mm) to 1⁄4″ (6mm) apart (A).

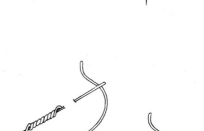

Bullion stitch

Bring the needle to the right side of the fabric. Take a stitch the length desired, bringing the needle up where the thread first came up from the wrong side, but do not pull the needle through. Wrap the thread around the point of the needle as many times as required (usually 6 or 7 times) (B). Holding your thumb on the wrapped needle, push the needle and thread end through both the fabric and the thread wrap, tightening the stitch by pulling on the thread end. Insert the needle back into the fabric as shown (C).

Chain stitch

On the design line, bring the needle up from the wrong side. Make a small loop with the thread in front of the needle, holding it in place with your thumb. Insert the needle into the fabric where you first brought it up and bring it out at the beginning of the next stitch, anchoring the top of the loop under the needle as it comes out (D).

Couching stitch

Holding the cord to be couched on the design line, take small stitches over the cord at 1⁄8″ to 1⁄4″ (3mm to 6mm) intervals—a shorter interval if the cord is to be very curved, the longer if it is straight or only slightly curved (E).

Cross stitch

Working from right to left, bring the needle up from the wrong side at the lower right corner of the stitch (1). Take a diagonal stitch across the weave, inserting the needle into the upper left-hand corner of the stitch (2) and coming out at the lower right corner of the next stitch (3), keeping the needle vertical. Continue in this manner until the row is complete. Then, bring the needle up from the lower left-hand corner of the last stitch back to the upper right, forming a cross (4). Continue, bringing the needle out at the lower left of the next stitch (5) and working from left to right back across the row (F).

French knot

Bring the needle up from the wrong side of the fabric. Holding the thread taut in your left hand, wind it twice around the needle, keeping the needle almost flat against the fabric. Insert the needle back into the fabric very close to where you first brought it up. Pull the thread gently through, forming the knot (G).

Gobelin stitch

Starting at the bottom of the stitch, bring the needle up from the wrong side of the canvas. Insert the needle straight above, as many weaves up as indicated by your design. Bring the needle back up beside the first stitch to begin the next stitch (H).

Satin stitch

Bring the needle up from the wrong side at the edge of the area to be filled in and at one end of the shape. Insert it on the opposite edge. Continue, making sure the stitches are smooth and close together (I).

Stem or Outline stitch

Bring the needle up from the wrong side on the *left* end of the design line. Insert it on the design line a short distance from where you first brought the needle up, bringing it out at the end of the previous stitch (J).
  For curved lines, keep the thread below the needle. For straight lines, keep the thread above the needle.

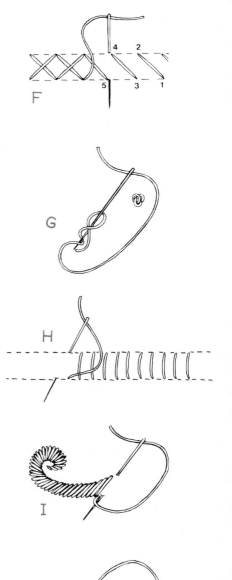

Straight stitch

Bring the needle up from the wrong side at one end of the design line and back down at the other end, coming up at an end of the next stitch (K).

THREADS

Your project instructions will tell you what kind and how many strands of embroidery thread, or floss, to use. There are, however, several different types of embroidery threads you may want to consider:

Embroidery floss

This has 6 strands that can be used singly or in any combination. It comes in shiny cotton, matte cotton, or very shiny crimped rayon, and all are suitable for most types of embroidery on almost any fabric, from sheer to heavy weight.

Perle cotton

Nos. 5 and 8 are smooth threads of medium thickness that work especially well with counted cross stitch. Perle cotton can be used on light to heavy weight fabrics.

Crewel yarn

Embroidery with this three-stranded yarn is called crewel work. Crewel yarn creates a thicker, more raised effect than the embroidery and perle cotton threads, and works well on medium to heavy weight fabrics.

Narrow satin ribbon

Instead of thread consider using satin ribbon ⅛" (3mm) and ¹⁄₁₆" (2mm) wide, which is suitable for embroidery on medium to heavy weight fabrics. While the ribbon tends to twist as you work, embroidery is faster with ribbon.

NEEDLES

The specific purpose of the needle, beside being a generally good way to get thread on fabric, is to make the correct size hole in

your fabric for the thread to go through. Match the point of the needle to the work and fabric, and make sure your thread or yarn can be easily inserted into the eye of your needle. Although whatever needle works well for you is your best choice, here are the three basic types designed for embroidery:

Crewel

Used with most types of embroidery threads, crewel needles are long and sharp, with a long thin eye.

Tapestry

With a blunt point and a long rounded eye, these needles are used with thicker threads and yarn for counted thread work on coarse fabrics, and for needlepoint on canvas.

Chenille

A bit shorter than the tapestry needle, with a long wide eye and a sharp point, chenille needles are used for embroidery with thicker threads and yarn on almost any type of fabric.

EMBROIDERY HOOPS

An embroidery hoop is actually two hoops, one fitting snugly inside the other, that holds the fabric in tightly between them. This tension creates a taut surface on which to embroider.

Hoops are made of wood, metal, or plastic, and available in round or oval shapes, from a few inches (centimeters) in diameter to more than 12" (30.5cm) across. There are large ones created especially for quilting. If you do a lot of embroidery, you may find that having several different sizes at hand gives you maximum flexibility.

Enlarging Patterns

Patterns are given on a grid when the full size of a piece exceeds the dimensions of the printed page. The grid serves as a measure and guide to enlarge your pattern to the correct size. Any large sheet of paper will do for your enlarged pattern. Or you can use graph paper, available at art supply or art needlework shops.

Start with the scale of the grid. If the scale is 1 square = 1" (25mm), you will need to draw a full-size grid of as many 1" (25mm) squares as there are on the smaller grid for each piece you want to enlarge. For instance, if the pattern piece covers an area on the grid of 4 squares across by 5 squares high, you create a full-size grid of 4 one-inch (25mm) squares by 5 one-inch (25mm) squares.

Next, copy the design on your full-size grid, square by square. Include all pattern markings and placement lines as you draw the full-size pattern.

When you have finished making the pattern, cut out all the pieces and make sure they fit together properly before you cut the pattern from fabric. If the pieces do not match, check to see if you copied the small pattern correctly to your full-size grid. Alter or redraw any faulty pieces.

CORNER GUIDES

Some projects call for fabric squares or rectangles with curved corners. For these, the dimensions are given along with a guide for the curved corner. Trace the curved corner guide for your project onto tracing paper. Cut out the corner along the outer curved edge. After you have cut out your squares and/or rectangles to the dimensions specified, place the corner guide at each corner and trace the curve. Cut your fabric along the curved corners.

Fabrics

Choosing fabric for a craft project is different from selecting fabric for a fashion garment. The important points to keep in mind are:

Weave

Choose firmly or tightly woven fabrics that do not ravel excessively. This is especially important when you are working with small projects and/or small pieces of fabric. Use woven fabrics unless knitted fabric is specified in the project.

Weight

Narrow seam allowances and intricate details in a small item call for light to medium weight fabrics. Conditions that permit heavier fabrics are wide seam allowances, gluing instead of sewing, mainly straight seams, and the fact that durability is required of the fabric.

Texture

Textured fabrics, such as velvet, velveteen, corduroy, brushed denim, chenille, as well as brocade, bouclé, and nubby weaves can be suitable for the project as long as the weight is appropri-ate. Make sure your fabric texture does not interfere with the design. For example, don't use a busy brocade for an intricate, finely seamed project. Most often, textured fabrics enhance craft projects.

Sensitivity to light and air

If your craft project is meant to be on permanent display or in constant use, fading or discoloration is a concern. Some satins are known to fade and discolor, and many white fabrics tend to yellow over a period of time. Often home gas heat or polluted air can cause fabrics to discolor, and sunlight can cause them to fade.

Design

In selecting fabrics, this is a matter of personal taste. Generally, the smaller the project, the smaller the print or surface design should be. Check to make sure the fabric design does not interfere with the project design. Avoid printed fabric that would camouflage delicate stitching, for example.

HELPFUL HINTS

■ Steam all your fabrics before you begin working with them. This will preshrink them and help raise any surface texture that may have been flattened. Test a scrap of your fabric first to make sure steam will not harm it. Do not steam or press metallic, beaded, or sequinned fabric, as the steam may tarnish the beads and sequins or melt the fabric.

■ If the craft project will be washed, then it is necessary to preshrink the trims as well.

■ If your project calls for fabrics to be glued, test the glue first to make sure it will not seep through and stain the right side of the fabric (see Adhesives, p. 10).

FELT

One of the most frequently used fabrics for crafts, felt is actually a formed rather than woven fabric. Tiny wool and/or synthetic (usually polyester or rayon) fibers are pressed together to form the felt. Felt does not ravel; its edges do not need finishing as the raw edges of woven fabrics do. It can be shaped with steam, and best of all, it is easy to work with.

Since felt has no grain, it can be cut in any direction. Use a very sharp shears or scissors, or if the felt is fairly stiff, you can use an X-acto knife. When cutting very small pieces, it is

especially important that your scissors are sharp, to avoid uneven edges. Buttonhole scissors or embroidery scissors work best for cutting small pieces of felt.

Sew felt with no more than 8 or 10 stitches per inch (per 25mm), as the holes created by the stitching may weaken the seam.

Felt takes well to glue, but always test-glue swatches to make sure the glue does not soak through and stain the right side of the felt.

IMITATION FUR AND FURLIKE FABRICS

Pattern pieces for imitation furs and high-pile fabrics must all be laid out in the same direction. Use transparent or masking tape to hold the pattern pieces in place on the wrong side of the fabric, and cut only one layer at a time.

Cut out high-pile fabrics with a single-edged razor blade, a mat knife, or an X-acto knife instead of scissors. Scissors can accidentally cut off some fur or pile. To cut, lift the fabric off the cutting surface with one hand and with the blade or knife in the other hand, make downward cuts. Apply even pressure to the fabric with the blade. Cut smoothly—do not cut around notches. Use chalk or a soft lead pencil to mark pattern notches and other symbols on the back of the fabric.

Sizes 14, 16, and 18 machine needles, regular point or all-purpose, are fine for sewing furry fakes. Of course, the size of the needle depends on the thickness of the fur. Thin fur or short pile requires a size 14 needle, and thicker, longer furs require a size 16 or 18 needle. Cotton-wrapped polyester, nylon, or heavy-duty mercerized cotton threads work well for fake furs, again with the heavier furs needing the heavier threads.

Fake fur can be difficult to pin together for stitching. Instead of standard straight pins, use paper clips or bobby pins, removing them as you come to them. When sewing by machine, loosen the pressure on the presser foot if you can, and use a medium stitch length—8 to 10 stitches per inch (per 25mm). Test-sew some scraps to make sure the pressure, thread tension, thread, and needle size all work. After stitching, use the point of a pin or needle to pull out any hairs or pile caught in the stitching (A).

A

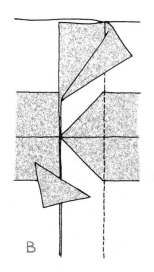

B

For seams that intersect, trim away as much pile as possible from the seam allowances, and trim the corners diagonally before the two seams are joined (B). This will prevent the right side from looking lumpy.

When sewing a layer of fake fur to a regular piece of fabric, take these simple precautions to avoid slipping and puckering. Baste the fake fur to the fabric, trim the fur off the seam allowance, then pull the remaining fur out of the seam. Then, stitch the seam, with the regular fabric up, in the direction of the fur's nap, if there is one.

IMITATION LEATHER AND SUEDE

On a single layer of fabric, lay out all your pattern pieces on the wrong side of the fabric in the same direction, as for fake furs. Follow the grainline on the backing, if there is one, and the nap on fake suedes. Use transparent or masking tape to hold the pattern pieces in place.

If the fabric is fairly thick, use a single-edged razor blade or X-acto knife to cut out your pattern. For thinner fabrics, use sharp shears. Cut through the tape as you go, and if cutting with shears, make even, continuous cuts, never fully closing the shears on each stroke, to get the smoothest line possible. Mark imitation leather and suede on the wrong side with chalk or a waterproof felt-tip pen.

When sewing by machine, use a special leather needle, available at fabric shops. Although not essential, this needle will make it easier for your machine to handle these materials. Use a size 11 or 14 leather or regular point needle, depending on the thickness of the fabric. Silk, heavy-duty mercerized cotton, and cotton-covered polyester thread will work well for both machine and hand sewing.

Test-stitch on scraps to check thread tension and presser foot pressure. Reduce the presser foot pressure if the material is not moving smoothly through the machine. If loosening the pressure does not help, place a strip of tissue paper between the presser foot and the material, between the material and the feed dog, or in both places. Tear the tissue away after stitching. When the thread tension is too tight, the seams will pucker, and the tight threads could tear the material. Loose tension results in stitches showing on opened seams.

Use a stitch length of 8 to 10 stitches per inch (per 25mm). Do not use pins to hold layers together for stitching. Instead, use paper clips or hair clips, removing them as you come to them. Masking tape can be used as well—it can be stitched over and removed when the seam is finished. But before using it, test to make sure it will not harm your material when it is peeled off.

Do not backstitch at the end of a seam, as you may weaken the seam or tear the material. Knot all thread ends and trim.

Avoid pressing imitation leathers and suedes, as an iron could melt some of them. Glue or pound seam allowances flat if necessary. If you absolutely must press, test-press scraps with a warm iron, using brown paper or a press cloth to protect the material.

Felt
See **Fabrics**

Fiberfill
See **Stuffing**

Fleece
See **Batting**

French Knot
See **Embroidery**

Fur and Furlike Fabric
See **Fabrics**

Fusible Interfacing
See **Interfacing**

Fusible Web
See **Adhesives**

Gathering

BY HAND

Gathering is done by hand on small pieces with very narrow seam allowances, ¼" (6mm) or less, and on very sheer or delicate fabrics. Use an unknotted doubled thread. Twenty-four inches (61cm) is a good length.

Make ⅛" to ¼" (3mm to 6mm) running stitches (see Hand Sewing, p. 34) in the seam allowance or on the gathering line, leaving a 5" to 6" (12.5cm to 15cm) "tail" of thread at both ends.

Pin the piece to be gathered to the shorter one, matching any seams and markings. Pull up the gathers to fit, distributing the fullness evenly and holding the gathers in place with more pins. Wind the ends of the thread around a pin in figure eights to hold the ends in place. Stitch with the gathered side up, removing the pins as you come to them. If the gathers are at an edge, gently press them in the seam allowance only.

BY MACHINE

This type of gathering works for fabrics with seam allowances of ⅜" (10mm) or wider.

Set your stitch length at 6–8 stitches per inch (per 25mm), and loosen the tension slightly. Make a row of gathering stitches on the seamline, leaving 4" to 5" (10cm to 12.5cm) "tails" of thread at each end. Do not backstitch. Make a second row of gathering stitches ¼" (6mm) away, in the seam allowance. Using 2 rows of gathering stitches makes it easier to control the gathers.

If lightweight fabrics pucker when you begin stitching, hold the fabric taut with one hand behind the needle, and with the other hand hold the fabric in front of the needle.

Pin the area to be gathered to the shorter area, matching markings. Proceed as for hand gathering, pulling up the gathers with the bobbin threads.

To distribute the fullness evenly when gathering, divide the length to be gathered and the area it will be sewn to into four or more equal sections. Mark the sections with safety pins or large straight pins. Sew separate rows of gathering stitches for each of the sections. Pin the layers together matching markings and proceed as for hand gathering.

Another method for gathering long lengths, especially for heavy fabrics, is to gather over a piece of cord. Cut a piece of strong, thin cord slightly longer than the section to be gathered. Set your machine for a zigzag stitch wide enough to stitch over the cord. Zigzag over the cord in the seam allowance, next to the seamline, taking care not to catch the cord in the stitching. Pin the zigzagged piece to the shorter one, matching markings. Wrap one end of the cord around a pin in a figure eight to secure it. Pull the other end of the cord to gather up the fabric. Distribute the gathers evenly and stitch, being careful again not to catch the cord in the stitching. Pull out the cord after the stitching is complete.

Gobelin Stitch
See **Embroidery**

Grosgrain Ribbon
See **Ribbons**

Hand Sewing

Backstitch

From the back, bring the needle to the right side of the fabric. Take a stitch back from 1/16" to 1/8" (2mm to 3mm), bringing the needle out on the right side 1/16" to 1/8" ((2mm to 3mm) beyond the beginning of the first stitch. Repeat, inserting the needle into the end of the last stitch and bring it out one stitch ahead. The stitches on the back will be twice as long as the ones on the right side (A).

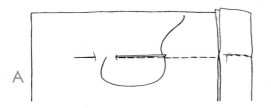

Catchstitch

Used to hold batting and interfacing in place and wherever some flexibility is needed, the catchstitch is worked from *left* to *right*, with the needle always pointing to the left. To begin,

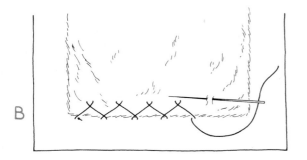

take a small stitch in the fabric at the edge of the batting. Next, take another small stitch about 1/4" (6mm) up and to the right of the first stitch, in the batting. Take the next small stitch down and to the right, in the fabric. Continue in this manner, alternating stitches from fabric to batting (B).

Overcast stitch

Used mainly to finish raw edges to prevent raveling, overcasting can also be used to hold two edges together. Going from right to left or from left to right, bring the needle to the right side from the back of your work at a point about 1/4" (6mm) from the edge. Holding the needle at a slight slant, space your stitches 1/4" (6mm) to 1/2" (13mm) apart (C).

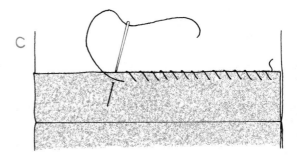

Running stitch

This simple, basic stitch is created by weaving the needle in and out of the fabric evenly, taking several stitches at one time before pulling the thread through. For fine, permanent seam-

ing or mending, make stitches ¹⁄₁₆″ (2mm) to ⅛″ (3mm) long; for hand gathering, ⅛″ to ¼″ (3mm to 6mm) long. Hand basting is a running stitch done with ¼″ (6mm) to ½″ (13mm) stitches (D).

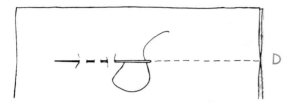

Slipstitch

Used for closing openings, attaching hand appliqués, and sewing trims in place, this stitch provides a practically invisible finish. Slide the needle about ¼″ (6mm) through the folded edge, picking up a thread or two of the underlayer where the needle comes out. Make stitches ⅛″ to ¼″ (3mm to 6mm). Use longer stitches for heavy or bulky fabrics (E).

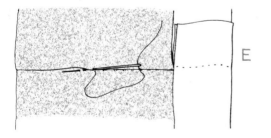

Tack

Take a small stitch on the back of the item being tacked. Take another small stitch into the fabric the item is being tacked to, drawing the two layers together. Take another two or three small stitches on each side, folding back the

fabric as necessary to make the stitches. The stitches should not be visible from the right side.

Whipstitch

These tiny, slanted stitches are used to trim or to hold two finished edges together. From the back of your work, insert the needle at a right angle to the edge, bringing the needle out ¹⁄₁₆″ (2mm) to ⅛″ (3mm) below the edge. The thread will enclose the edge. Make stitches ¹⁄₁₆″ (2mm) apart or closer together (F).

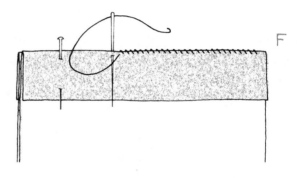

HELPFUL HINTS

■ Use beeswax to strengthen your thread and to prevent tangling. It is available in handy holders that the thread can be drawn through.

■ Cut thread ends diagonally. Then, thread the needle with the cut end of the thread. Knot this end as well.

■ If you find using a thimble is difficult, purchase a rubber fingertip protector from an office supply store. The rubber tip gives you more flexibility and is more comfortable to use.

Interfacing

FUSIBLE

A marvelous time-saver, fusible interfacing gives support and stability to those areas of your project where it is used. Available by the yard or in pre-packaged amounts, you'll find fusibles in woven, non-woven, and knitted types, and in sheer to heavy weights. Whether you choose a woven or non-woven interfacing is up to you, as long as the fabric and interfacing are compatible. Fusibles can be used safely on most fabric types except some silks, very lightweight fabrics, seersucker, fabrics that can be harmed by heat or steam, or those heavily textured on both sides. Always test the fusible interfacing on a scrap of fabric before fusing it onto your project pieces.

Fusible interfacings often are stretchable in one direction, stable in the other. Check the bolt end or your package instructions for complete information. Cut the fusible interfacing for your project so that it will make the best use of the most stable direction.

After you've cut the fusible interfacing pieces you need, trim off the seam allowance to within ⅛" (3mm) of the seamline. To reduce bulk, trim corners diagonally. Place the fusible side, which is usually shiny, on the wrong side of the piece to be interfaced. If the piece is large, "fuse baste" it in place at the edges every 3" to 4" (7.5cm to 10cm) with the tip of your iron. When you are satisfied with the placement, follow manufacturer's directions to permanently fuse the interfacing in place.

SEW-IN

This type of interfacing is available in woven and non-woven versions, both in a wide range of weights, by the yard or in prepackaged amounts. Unlike fusible interfacing, sew-in types can be used on all fabrics.

Sew-in interfacing, like fusible interfacing, often has one stable direction and one that may have some stretch. The bolt end or package instructions will tell you about the brand you are buying. For craft items, cut the sew-in interfacing following the most stable direction.

Pin the interfacing to the wrong side of your fabric pieces, trimming any corners diagonally. Machine baste the interfacing ⅛" (3mm) away from the seamline in the seam allowance. Trim the interfacing close to the stitching.

Jacquard Ribbon
See **Ribbons**

Lace

Flat

Flat lace is ungathered lace. It may have one straight edge and one scalloped edge, two straight edges, or two scalloped edges. If it is to be sewn on top of another layer for a trim, look for lace that has two straight or two scalloped sides. If it is to be gathered and inserted into a seam, look for flat lace with one straight edge and one scalloped edge. The straight edge is the one you gather (see Gathering, p. 33).

Pregathered

This type of lace comes with one edge already gathered and bound. It saves time and is easy to use, but the gathered fullness is minimal.

Beading

This is a flat eyelet-type lace with holes in it for ribbon to be woven through the openings.

Frequently beading can be found with ruffled edges or prewoven with ribbon.

SEWING LACE

To use as a trim on top of another layer of fabric, sew flat lace down along both long edges. Sew pregathered lace along its bound edge. Pregathered lace will follow curves easily, while flat lace will not, unless it is less than ½" (13mm) wide. To turn corners, see Corners for Trims, p. 24.

When your project requires inserting gathered lace into a seam, your pattern instructions specify exactly where it should be positioned in the seam allowance so it is completely hidden when the seam is sewn. Generally you match the gathering line of flat lace to the seamline, or place the bound edge of the pregathered type just above the seamline. Baste both types in place, then proceed with the seam.

If the lace ends are to be joined, you can either do a French seam (see Drawstring Gift Bag, step 5, p. 104) or a double-stitched one (see Heart Sachet, step 1, p. 92). If your lace is fairly sheer, you can overlap the ends, matching the design and the scallops on the edge. Using a narrow zigzag stitch with a short stitch length, stitch down the center of the overlap. Trim off the excess lace on both sides close to the stitching and you will have an almost invisible seam.

Make a narrow hem on gathered lace ends that are not joined to each other, unless specified otherwise by your project instructions. Turn under the raw end ¼" (6mm). Turn under again ¼" (6mm) and machine stitch or hand slipstitch the hem in place.

Leather and Suede
See **Fabrics**

Machine Stitching

Seam allowances on craft projects are often narrower than those found on clothing, often ⅜″ (10mm) or ¼″ (6mm). Follow your project instructions for the proper width of seam allowance. Make sure your stitch settings and thread tensions are correct for the materials you are sewing, and make a test seam on scraps of fabric before you begin sewing.

NARROW SEAMS

Remember these tips when sewing narrow seams:

■ Use a small-hole needle plate if you are not using a zigzag stitch. The small hole will prevent the fabric from accidentally getting pushed down into the machine by the needle.

■ Hold the thread ends as you begin stitching the seam. This will prevent the thread from bunching up and snarling the edges of the fabric.

■ Use the edge of your zigzag presser foot as a seam guide for ¼″ (6mm) seams.

STITCHING TECHNIQUES

Backstitch

Take a few stitches in reverse at the beginning of a seam, holding the thread ends behind the needle. This will secure the threads at the beginning of the seam and prevent it from coming apart.

Edgestitch

To stabilize and trim a finished edge, straight stitch very close to the edge, turning the flywheel by hand as you pivot around corners. Use a small-hole needle plate to prevent edges and corners from being jammed down into the machine.

Staystitch

This simple sewing procedure is important to all types of sewing and should not be neglected when you sew crafts. It prevents stretching and also serves as a guideline when clipping curves. Using a short stitch length, 10–12 stitches per inch (per 25mm), stitch in the direction of the grain just inside the seamline in the seam allowance.

EDGE FINISHES

Zigzag stitching

As a seam finish zigzag stitching can be done in one of two ways: (1) Zigzag through both layers of fabric close to the stitched seam, then trim the seam allowance close to the zigzagged stitching. This is a good seam finish for light to medium weight fabrics; or (2) zigzag each edge of the seam allowance and press it open. This method works well with medium to heavy weight fabrics.

As an edge finish, zigzagged stitching can be used by itself to create a satin stitched edge, much the way buttonhole stitching looks. It is a pretty alternative to the traditional narrow hem and can be used on any weight fabric. It is not recommended for loosely woven fabrics.

Straight stitch a line ¼″ (6mm) in from the edge you want to satin stitch to stabilize it. Then, set your machine at a narrow width zigzag stitch and at a very short stitch length to get the stitches close together. Test on a scrap of fabric to see if the settings are suitable. Satin stitch over the line of straight stitching, turning corners and curves as for appliqués (see p. 12). Trim off excess fabric close to the stitching.

NARROW HEM

A narrow hem is the traditionally tidy edge finish for light to medium weight fabrics. It works on gentle curves as well as on straight edges. Trim the hem allowance to ½" (13mm). Turn under ¼" (6mm), press, then turn under ¼" (6mm) again and press. Stitch close to the fold. For corners, turn up ¼" (6mm) and press. Trim off the ¼" turn-up diagonally across the corners. Turn up ¼" (6mm) again and press, forming a miter in the corner. Stitch close to the fold (A).

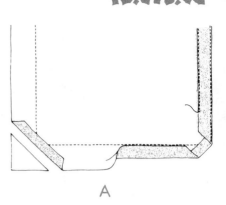

A

Mat Board

Stiffer and thicker than poster board, mat board is usually used to create borders around pictures and artwork. In a craft project mat board offers extra support and stiffness that poster board does not give. It can be purchased in art supply or craft stores. Since it is sturdier than poster board be sure to ask specifically for mat board.

Because mat board is too thick and stiff to be cut with scissors, it must be cut with a mat knife or X-acto knife, both of which may also be purchased in art supply and craft stores. A mat knife is a sharp blade in a safety handle, similar in shape to a carpet knife, and its blades can be replaced when dulled. An X-acto knife is smaller, is

held in the hand and used like a pencil, and also has replaceable blades. Never attempt to use a razor blade to cut mat board. It is too stiff to be cut with a razor blade and you may hurt yourself.

With a pencil, mark off or trace the pattern pieces to be cut. With the mat knife or X-acto knife, score (lightly cut) the surface of the board, following the pencil lines. Working on a well-padded surface, cover the tabletop with thick cardboard or magazines, cut the mat board along the scored lines. You may find it easier to hold the board slightly off the work surface with one hand while you cut with the other.

Smooth any rough edges with an emery board or fine sandpaper.

Narrow Hem
See **Machine Stitching**

Outline Stitch
See **Embroidery**

Overcast Stitch
See **Hand Sewing**

Polyester Fiberfill
See **Stuffing**

Quilting by Machine

You can purchase prequilted fabrics for many projects that call for quilted fabrics or you can quilt your own. You will need enough fabric for the project, an equal amount of batting or fleece, and the same amount of backing fabric. The backing fabric may be muslin, the same as the top fabric, or a contrasting fabric—which can be attractive if the item has no lining. The fabric is quilted before the pattern pieces are cut.

PREPARATION

Cut the piece of fabric to be quilted, the batting or fleece, and the backing fabric all the same size, allowing at least a 1″ (25mm) clearance around all edges of the pattern piece or pieces that will be cut from the quilted fabric. The quilting decreases the square area of the fabric as it becomes thicker from the addition of batting and backing. Use a ruler and a soft lead pencil or dressmaker's chalk pencil to mark your quilting lines on your fabric. If you have a quilting foot, you need mark only the first two rows that cross the center of your fabric. Your quilting foot will guide you in sewing the remaining rows.

On a flat surface, spread out the backing, wrong side up. Place the batting or fleece on top of the backing. Smooth the batting out carefully. Place the wrong side of the marked top, also known as the face fabric, over the batting, creating a three-layered sandwich of fabric. You are now ready to baste the layers together, which is *the* most important part of quilting. The more you baste, the less likely the layers are to shift when you are quilting. Do not hesitate to add more rows of basting rather than less, because the results you get will be directly related to how well you have basted the to-be-quilted layers. Beginning in the center, baste lengthwise, then crosswise, then diagonally to all 4 corners (A). Add more rows in any direction, starting from the center out. Finally, baste around the edges.

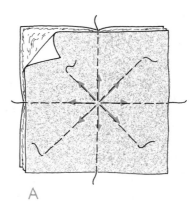

A

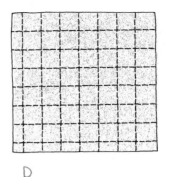

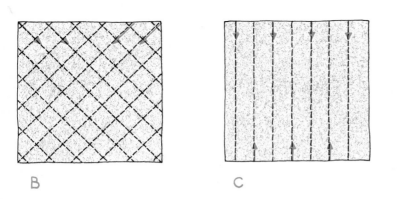

B   C   D

SEWING

There are several traditional ways to machine quilt your fabric: diamond (B), channel (C), and square (D). You may also invent your own pattern. For the types shown here, a machine quilting foot will make the job easier. The foot has a bar, used as a guide, that can be adjusted so your stitching rows are evenly spaced. After you decide which design you want and how far apart the rows of stitching, set the quilting foot at the proper distance.

Sew using no more than a medium length stitch setting of 8 to 10 stitches per inch (per 25mm). Make some stitching tests on scraps of fabric and batting. Use matching or contrasting thread, and begin stitching with the rows that cross the center. Alternate directions each time you start a new row. For example, if you are doing diamond quilting, stitch the first row from corner to corner, crossing the center. Stitch the second row perpendicular to the first, again crossing the center, then the next row in the same direction as the first, the third parallel to the second, and so on until the entire piece is quilted. For channel quilting, begin each row on the edge where you ended the previous row.

Cut your pattern piece from the quilted fabric.

Ribbons

Always buy quality ribbon for your craft projects. Since it is very visible as a trim, fine ribbon can only add to your project's appeal. There are two categories of ribbon to consider—craft ribbon and fashion ribbon.

CRAFT RIBBON

Often called cut-edge ribbon, it is usually made from fabric that has been coated, then cut into ribbon widths. It is not washable and not good for sewing, but can be glued easily. It is used for bows for floral arrangements, gift wrap, and other decorative applications. Your project will specify this type of ribbon if it can be used.

FASHION RIBBON

Versatile, beautiful, and durable, fashion ribbon is used as a sew-on trim (it can be glued as well). It is usually machine washable (check the bolt end). Fashion ribbon is woven and, therefore, has its own selvage, and you'll find it available in different types: grosgrain, jacquard, satin, and velvet, each of which has its own characteristics:

Grosgrain

This ribbon has a ribbed weave and a soft surface finish and no wrong side. It is good as an edgestitched trim and is especially suitable for ribbon ties, bows, and zipper pulls because it stays in place when tied or knotted.

Jacquard

This is a very pretty, elegant trim with its woven-in designs. It has a right side and a wrong side, and works best as an edgestitched trim.

Satin

With its smooth, shiny surface, satin ribbon is an especially pretty ribbon trim. It can be either single faced, with one right side and one wrong side, or double faced, with two right sides. Use it as an edgestitched trim, for decorative bows, to make flowers, or in lace or eyelet beading.

Velvet

Lush, crush-free and rich-looking, velvet ribbon has a selvage on both edges for easy stitching. It should be treated like napped fabric: when using more than one parallel row of velvet ribbon, make sure the nap in each row is going in the same direction. It may be used as an edgestitched trim or for decorative bows.

SEWING RIBBON

Before sewing, steam ribbon thoroughly to preshrink, if necessary. Use a new regular point needle, size 11 or 14, and a stitch length setting of 10 to 12 stitches per inch (per 25mm). Test-sew a bit of ribbon onto some scraps of fabric to check your machine settings. To keep the ribbon from puckering, always stitch both sides of the ribbon in the same direction.

Pin your ribbon along any placement lines or in the position you want. Sew ribbon as you would for braid, p. 23. To turn corners, see p. 24.

GLUING RIBBON

Gluing is an easy way to apply ribbon. All you have to do is be sure that the glue will not soak through the ribbon and stain the right side. Test-glue some samples first. (See Adhesives, p. 10.)

RIBBON AS A ZIPPER PULL

For a zipper pull use an 8″ (20.5cm) length of ⅜″ (10mm) grosgrain ribbon. Fold the ribbon in half crosswise and pull about 1″ (25mm) of the folded end through the hole in the end of the zipper pull. Bring the raw ends through the ribbon loop and pull tightly.

Running Stitch
See **Hand Sewing**

Satin Ribbon
See **Ribbons**

Satin Stitch
See **Embroidery**

Sequins
See **Beads**

Sew-in Interfacing
See **Interfacing**

Slipstitch
See **Hand Sewing**

Staystitch
See **Machine Stitching**

Stem Stitch
See **Embroidery**

Straight Stitch
See **Embroidery**

Stuffing

POLYESTER FIBERFILL

Readily available and packaged in bags holding from 12 oz. to 24 oz. (340g to 680g) or more, polyester fiberfill is inexpensive, versatile, washable, may be dry cleaned, and is easy to handle.

To stuff small items, pull off tufts of stuffing about the size of cotton balls, as larger ones could make the item lumpy. Using the eraser end of a pencil, push the small tufts of stuffing into the areas and corners of the item that your fingers can't reach. Make sure all the curves and shaped areas of your project are firmly stuffed. Continue stuffing the item with small tufts of fiberfill.

For larger projects, first stuff with small tufts of stuffing the small areas your fingers can't reach, using a ruler or the eraser end of a pencil. Push the small tufts in firmly, arranging the stuffing so it is smooth. Then use slightly larger tufts in the larger areas of your project, packing it firmly and smoothly.

Generally pillows do not need to be stuffed as firmly as toys and other items. To stuff pillows and other large items push small tufts of stuffing into corners and curved areas, again using the eraser end of a pencil. Stuff the rest of the cavity with tufts of fiberfill slightly smaller than your fist.

OTHER TYPES OF STUFFING

Foam is an alternative to fiberfill. It can be messy, and can crumble into dust after a few years. It is, however, cheaper than fiberfill and is usually washable, but not dry cleanable. Push the foam into corners and other areas as for fiberfill.

Worn-out nylon stockings and pantihose are often used as stuffing. For small items, cut into small pieces and push into corners and other areas as for fiberfill.

Styrofoam

Used as a basic shape for wreaths and ornaments, this is a lightweight synthetic material that needs to be handled carefully. It can be easily damaged or broken if too much surface pressure is applied to it, so never squeeze it or stack a lot of heavy items on top of it.

Attach fabrics, trims, and other materials with straight pins. Position pins carefully and push them into the Styrofoam at an angle. After you have determined that the placement of the trims is correct, remove each pin with the trim on it and put a tiny drop of white glue on the point of each pin. Carefully reinsert the pin into the same hole. When you remove the pin, the hole remains, so plan carefully.

Tapes and glues do not adhere well to the surface of Styrofoam. Avoid them when you can.

Make sure trims you pin on the Styrofoam are not so heavy that they will not stay pinned in place.

If you must cut the Styrofoam, use a sharp knife or blade. Do not use shears. Cut slowly to avoid jagged edges.

Tack
See **Hand Sewing**

Threads

For crafts, almost any good quality thread is suitable. Stay away from poor quality threads, as they can make sewing unpleasant. Stick with thread brand names that are well known. Here are some helpful hints:

■ Cotton thread doesn't tangle. If your project calls for a lot of hand sewing, consider this type of thread.

■ Nylon thread does not hold a knot. Use clear nail polish to keep the knotted ends secure.

■ Silk thread is especially good for basting. It will not leave "thread marks" on your fabrics, and slides in and out of your fabric easily.

SPECIAL THREADS

Buttonhole twist is used for topstitching and hand-sewn buttonholes.

Metallic thread adds a lovely touch for decorative hand and machine sewing.

Quilting thread is used for hand and machine quilting.

Topstitching thread is used for topstitching and decorative stitching.

When you are shopping for special and novelty threads, always buy brand names. The better known brands are generally a better quality, which means that the thread will be easier to use. Poor quality novelty threads can break easily,

making it difficult to use them for hand sewing and practically impossible to use on your machine.

Before stitching, especially with a thread you are not familiar with, test-stitch on scraps of fabric to check the thread tension. Some sewing machines will not handle some of the special threads, such as the metallics, and if this is the case for you, be sure to have an alternative stitching plan. Check your machine manual for the proper adjustments to make.

Transferring Designs

There are many ways to transfer embroidery and beading motifs or other designs to your fabric. The method you use has a lot to do with the type of fabric you are using.

First, trace the design (either the pattern's or your own) onto tracing paper (available at art supply or art needlework shops), then transfer the design to your fabric using one of the methods listed below.

Depending on the transfer method you choose, you will have to be aware that care must be taken in transferring designs that are not reversible; that is, if you hold the design up to a mirror and it is backwards, such as some monograms, your transfer must be reversed.

Since most craft projects will not be washed and some transfer mediums are permanent (such as some transfer pencils), be doubly sure your lines are correct and that your needlework completely covers them.

DRESSMAKER'S CARBON PAPER AND TRACING WHEEL

This method will work on any smooth-surfaced fabric. Sandwich a piece of carbon paper face down between your fabric and the tracing paper. Follow the outline on the tracing paper with the tracing wheel to transfer the design to your fabric.

TRANSFER TRACING PAPER AND PEN

Available at needlework and fabric shops, this is a special type of tracing paper. When the design is traced with the special pen that comes with it, the tracing can be rubbed directly onto the fabric. This is a good technique for transferring designs onto felt and other soft fabrics. However, if the design is not reversible, such as some letters of the alphabet, trace the design first on regular tracing paper. Then, turn the tracing paper over and trace the reversed design onto the transfer tracing paper. The design will be in reverse, and when you put the transfer paper face down on your fabric the design will be transferred correctly.

TRANSFER PENCIL

Available in needlework and fabric stores, the transfer pencil can be used with any smooth-surfaced fabric. Trace the design onto tracing paper with the transfer pencil. Then, with a warm iron, transfer the design to the fabric. If the design is not reversible, trace it onto tracing paper with a regular pencil, then use the transfer pencil to retrace the reversed design on the back of the tracing paper. Transfer this side to the fabric.

TEAR-AWAY FABRIC

For textured or napped fabrics, such as velvet, raw silk, or nubby linen, trace the design onto a tear-away fabric made specially for appliqué and embroidery. Baste the tear-away fabric to the project fabric, and work the design. When finished, gently tear off the tear-away fabric. You'll find tear-away fabric in fabric and art needlework shops.

Velvet Ribbon
See **Ribbons**

Whipstitch
See **Hand Sewing**

White Glue
See **Adhesives**

Zigzag Stitching
See **Machine Stitching**

No-Sew Ribbon Ball Ornaments, *page 55*

Embroidered Felt Ornaments, *page 59*

Tree Skirt, *page 65*

Heirloom Treetop Angel, *page 50*

Santa Pillow, *page 79*

**Christmas Table
Decorations: Fabric Tree,
Table Runner, Placemats,
Napkins, Napkin Ring, and
Poinsettias,** *page 84*

Victorian Ornaments, *page 60*

Shirred Wreath, *page 71*

**Classic Christmas
Stocking,** *page 68*

Nosegay Wreath, *page 74*

Holiday Appliquéd Apron, *page 82*

Santa Christmas Card Holder, *page 88*

Fabric Basket, *page 77*

Casserole and Oven Mitts, *page 127*

Sleeping Baby, Carrier, and Coverlet, *page 113*

Quilted Tote, *page 96*

Needleworker's Carryall Tote, *page 101*

Cosmetic Case, *page 94*

Desk Accessories: Briefcase, Pencil Case, and Picture Frame, *page 118*

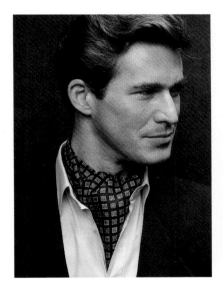

Tie, Cummerbund, and Ascot, *page 98*

Bed Caddy, *page 122*

Sachets, *page 92*

Padded Hanger and Hanger Cover, *page 124*

Drawstring Gift Bag, *page 104*

Cap'n Joshua Teddy Bear, *page 106*

Decorating the Tree

Heirloom Treetop Angel

Think back to your childhood memories of Christmas. Remember how tall the Christmas tree looked, topped with that majestic angel? Now you can create just such an angel for your own Christmas tree. Trimmed with lace and ribbon, it can become an heirloom to be used and enjoyed for many years. Wouldn't it be a shame, though, to enjoy this angel only at Christmas? Make this one of shimmering satin and lace, and then another with a linen dress and cotton apron for your children to enjoy all year long. Why not an entire family of angel dolls? Let your imagination guide you—the possibilities are practically endless.

Finished size: 10¼″ high × 8⅜″ wide (26cm × 21cm).

MATERIALS NEEDED

Pattern pieces are found on pp. 144-145.

Dress
⅜ yd (0.40m) of 35″ or 45″ (90cm or 115cm) fabric

Wings and apron
¼ yd (0.30m) of 35″ or 45″ (90cm or 115cm) contrast fabric

Head, face, neck base
6½″ × 9″ (17cm × 23cm) of pink, off-white *or* brown fabric remnant

Hands
1½″ × 2½″ (4cm × 7cm) pink, off-white *or* brown felt remnant

Trims and notions
3 yds (2.80m) of 1″ (25mm) flat eyelet
⅝ yd (0.60m) of ½″ (13mm) eyelet beading with lace ruffling
1½ yds (1.40m) of ¼″ (6mm) ribbon *or* novelty trim
¼ yd (0.30m) of ⅛″ (3mm) ribbon
red and black embroidery floss
6½″ × 9″ (17cm × 23cm) cardboard, *or* poster board, *or* oak tag
6″ × 7½″ (15cm × 19cm) remnant of polyester batting
one small skein each of wool *or* mohair yarn and metallic yarn for hair
polyester fiberfill for head

CUTTING INFORMATION

Fabric: 1 dress front; 2 dress backs; 2 sleeves
Contrast fabric: 2 wings; 2 aprons
Felt Remnant: 2 hands
Polyester batting: 1 wing
Cardboard: 1 body

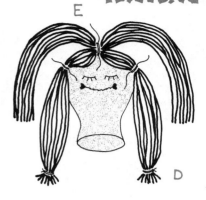

HOW-TO

All seam allowances are ⅜″ (10mm).

Head

1 Outline the face pattern on the fabric remnant. Transfer eye and mouth markings (see Transferring Designs, p. 47). With 3 strands of black floss, embroider lid lines in the stem stitch, and lashes in the straight stitch (see Embroidery, p. 25). With 3 strands of red floss, embroider the mouth curve in the stem stitch, and the corners of the mouth in the satin stitch (see Embroidery, p. 25). Cut out 1 face, 2 heads, and 1 neck base from the fabric remnant.

2 With right sides together, stitch the head sections at the center back. Stitch the face to the head with right sides together at the sides (A). Trim the seam and turn the head right side out.

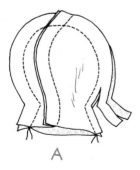

3 Turn in ⅜″ (10mm) at the neck opening. Baste and press. Stuff the head firmly with fiberfill (see Stuffing, p. 44) (B).

4 Stitch ⅜″ (10mm) from the raw edge at the neck base. Turn in along the stitching line, folding in the fullness as evenly as possible. Baste and press. Pin the neck base to the neck opening and slipstitch (see Hand Sewing, p. 34) the basted edges together (C).

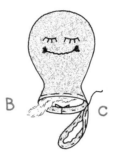

Hair

1 Cut 20 strands of regular yarn and 20 of metallic yarn, each 9″ (23cm) long. With ends even, tie all 40 pieces together in the center with a small piece of yarn.

2 On each side of the center, separate and tie 25 strands of yarn together, with a small strand of yarn 1″ (25mm) away from the center and another small strand ½″ (13mm) in from the ends (D). The remaining yarn will be used later.

3 Place the center of the hair at the center front of the head, just below the head seam. Tack (see Hand Sewing, p. 34) the hair at the center front and at the upper ties (E).

4 Bring the tied ends of yarn hair to the back of the head, positioning the ends on each side of the center back seam about halfway down the head. Tack the ends in place (F), keeping the remainder of the hair free.

5 Bring the remaining yarn hair over the head, arranging the strands so they cover the tacked ends. Tack the loose strands to the lower edge of the head, making sure the yarn forms a smooth surface across the back of the head (G).

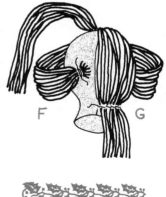

Body

1 Form the cardboard into a cone, lapping 1 edge to the placement line. Hold the cone in place with tape (H).

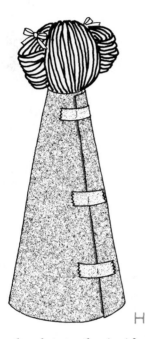

2 Apply glue to the inside top edge of the cone. Insert the head into the cone, with the taped edge at the back of the head.

3 Cut 2 pieces of ⅛" (3mm) ribbon, each 4" (10cm) long. Tie them into bows and tack the bows to the angel's hair over the side ties near the face.

Dress

1 Pin a felt hand, thumb down, to the short end of the right side of each sleeve between small •'s, with raw edges even. Baste (I).

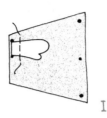

2 Fold each sleeve in half, right sides together. Stitch, leaving the wide end open. Trim the seam, turn to the right side, and press.

3 Pin each sleeve to the right side of the dress front at the sides, thumbs up, matching symbols. Baste (J).

4 Stitch the center back seam. Press the seam open. Stitch the front to the back at the sides, right sides together. Press the seams open, and turn the dress right side out.

5 Turn in the upper edge of the dress ¼" (6mm) to the inside. Sew in place by hand. Make 2 rows of hand gathering stitches (see Gathering, p. 33) ¼" (6mm) and again ½" (13mm) in from the folded edge (K).

6 Cut a piece of flat eyelet 36" (92cm) long. Stitch the ends together in a ¼" (6mm) seam to form a continuous loop. Press the seam open. Make 2 rows of hand gathering stitches, ⅜" (10mm) and ½" (13mm) from the straight edge.

J

52

7 With right sides together, pin the eyelet to the lower edge of the dress, placing the eyelet seam at the center back seam and having the raw edges even. Adjust the gathers evenly, and baste. Stitch. Turn the eyelet down. Press the seam allowance toward the dress (L).

8 Starting at the center back, pin the beading to the lower edge of the dress, centering it on the placement line, and lapping the ends ¼" (6mm). Sew the long edges and ends of the beading in place by hand (M).

9 Cut a piece of flat eyelet 22" (56cm) long. Gather it as you did with the dress eyelet. Turn under the ends ¼" (6mm) and

press. Pin the eyelet to the right side of one apron section, along the sides and lower edge, placing the ends at the small •'s. Adjust the gathers and baste (N).

10 Stitch the apron sections, right sides together, leaving the upper edge open. Trim the seam (O), turn to the right side, and press.

11 Turn in the seam allowances at the upper edge; baste. Slipstitch the basted edges together. Pin ¼" (6mm) ribbon or trim to the sides and lower edge of the apron, mitering the corners (see Corners for Trims, p. 24), and turning in ¼" (6mm) on the ends. Hand sew the trim or ribbon in place.

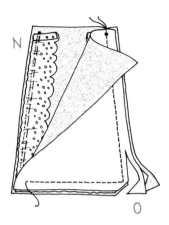

12 Pin the apron to the dress, placing the upper edge of the apron along the placement line, matching symbols. Tack at small •'s and the center front.

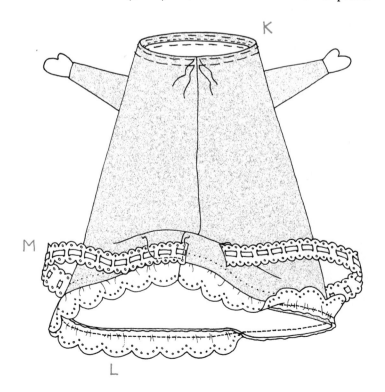

13 Slip the dress over the angel's head, placing the gathering along the upper edge of the cardboard. Adjust the gathers evenly around the body. Knot the ends of thread. Place the right hand over the left hand, in the front, and glue in place (P).

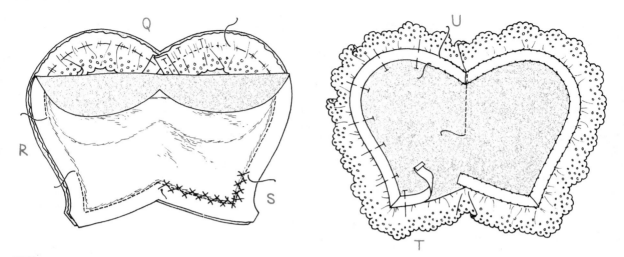

Wings

1 On the remaining eyelet trim, turn under the ends ¼″ (6mm) and press. Gather it as you did for the dress eyelet. Starting at the center of the upper edge, pin the eyelet to the right side of 1 wing section. Adjust the gathers evenly and baste (Q).

2 Stitch the wing sections, right sides together, leaving a 2″ (5cm) opening for turning (R). Trim seam.

3 Trim off the seam allowance from the batting and pin it to the wrong side of the wings. Catchstitch (see Hand Sewing, p. 34) the batting to the seam allowance (S).

4 Turn right side out and press. Slipstitch the opening. Starting at the center of the lower edge, pin the remaining ¼″ (6mm) ribbon to the outer edge of the wings, mitering the corners. Lap the ends ¼″ (6mm), sew in place by hand (T). Stitch the wings along the stitching line (U).

5 Pin the wings to the angel's back, with the ribbon side facing front. Place the stitching on the wings at the center of the head. Slipstitch the wings to the dress at the center back.

No-Sew Ribbon Ball Ornaments

Any of these 4 lovely ornaments can be yours without sewing a stitch. The easy-to-follow instructions will help you decorate your tree with a special flair. Although made here in the traditional Christmas colors of red and green, you can mix and match ribbons in your favorite colors. Even use different-textured ribbons for an interesting effect; try a velvet ribbon with a satin or metallic one. Or use a 6" (15cm) styrofoam ball, decorate it with ribbon, add a sprig of mistletoe—and you've got a kissing ball! If you are giving these ornaments as gifts, consider personalizing the hanging loop by embroidering it with the receiver's initials and your own, and the year, to serve as a memento of your friendship and love.

Finished size: approximately 2½" (65mm) in diameter.

BALL C
BALL B
BALL A
BALL D

MATERIALS NEEDED

For all 4 ornaments

1 box of 1" (25mm) straight pins (for lightweight ribbon)
1 box of 1¼" (32mm) silk pins (for heavyweight ribbon)
white craft glue (optional)
four 2½" (65mm) diameter Styrofoam balls

Ball A

1 yd (1.00m) of ⅜" (10mm) red ribbon
½ yd (0.50m) of ⅜" (10mm) green ribbon
1 yd (1.00m) of ⅜" (10mm) red print ribbon
1 yd (1.00m) of ⅝" (15mm) eyelet trim (with 1 straight and 1 scalloped edge)

Ball B

1 yd (1.00m) of ⅜" (10mm) red print ribbon
1⅝ yd (1.50m) of ⅜" (10mm) green print ribbon
2 yds (1.90m) of ½" (13mm) eyelet ruffling

Ball C

1¾ yds (1.60m) of ⅝" (15mm) red print ribbon with edging
1½ yds (1.40m) of ⅜" (10mm) red print ribbon
2 yds (1.90m) of ⅜" (10mm) green ribbon
2½ yds (2.30m) of ½" (13mm) eyelet trim with scalloped edges and small motif

Ball D

1⅞ yds (1.80m) of ⅝" (15mm) green print ribbon with edging
1⅞ yds (1.80m) of ⅜" (10mm) green ribbon
3 yds (2.80m) of ⅜" (10mm) red print ribbon

No pattern pieces are required.

GENERAL INFORMATION

■ Use a scrap of string, yarn, or heavy thread to divide the balls into quarters and/or eighths. Hold one end of the string against the ball, then wind the rest of the string around the ball twice, as you would to tie up a box. Anchor this marker in place with pins, slightly away from the center top and bottom, making sure the quarters are equal (A). For Ball C or D use a second color and repeat to divide the ball into eighths, placing the marker so it evenly divides the quarters.

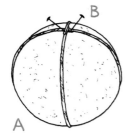

■ For greater stability always place pins at a slight angle rather than straight down (B). You can glue the pins in place after you have completed each ball, for a permanent finish. To do this, pull each pin up slightly, out of the ball but not out of the ribbon. Place a drop of glue in the pinhole underneath the ribbon. Push the pin back and hold it in place for a few seconds. Repeat for each pin.

■ Make a hanging loop for each ball from a 7" (18cm) length of ribbon. Select this ribbon to complement or contrast with the ornament. You can use anything from rickrack to velvet ribbons. If you have any remnants of lace seam binding, they will give your ornaments a delicate finishing touch. Overlap the cut ends and pin them in place on top of the ball. Test to see if the ball hangs properly. If not, repin the loop (C).

■ To make a finishing bow at the top of the ball, cut a 17" (43cm) length of ribbon and mark its center. Pin the center over the loop. Tie the ribbon into a bow and anchor it with a pin hidden in each loop. Trim the ribbon ends diagonally.

HOW-TO

Ball A

1 Cut 2 pieces of green ribbon and 4 pieces of red ribbon, each 8" (20.5cm) long. Divide the ball into quarters. Center the green ribbon over the quarter markers, lapping the ends slightly away from the top point (A).

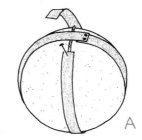

2 Starting at the top, wrap each piece of red ribbon around the ball, lapping it slightly over the edge of the green ribbon and crossing it at the bottom point (B), and continuing up the other side of the same green ribbon. Pin in place. Continue, so that each green ribbon is slightly overlapped on both sides by a red ribbon (C).

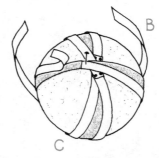

3 Cut 8 pieces of eyelet trim, each 4" (10cm) long. Starting at the top, pin a piece of trim in

place with the scalloped edge overlapping a red ribbon and the straight edge centered on an uncovered area of the ball. Line up another piece of eyelet trim, straight edge to straight edge, in the same manner, and pin in place (D). Repeat with the 6 remaining pieces of eyelet.

4 Cut 2 pieces of red print ribbon, each 8½" (21.5cm) long. Starting and ending at the top, center each red ribbon over the straight edges of the eyelet. Pin in place (E).

5 Make a hanging loop (see General Information, p. 56) of red print ribbon. Then use a 12" (30.5cm) piece of red print ribbon to make a bow and attach it according to the instructions on p. 56.

Ball B

1 Divide the ball into quarters, marking the top and bottom points with large hat pins. Divide the ball in half crosswise, using a tape measure to locate the halfway point on each quarter marker between the pins (A).

2 Cut 8 pieces of red print and 8 pieces of green print ribbons,

each 4" (10cm) long. Do not cut eyelet trim. Starting at the top, place the bound edge of the eyelet over quarter markers, pinning the eyelet in place near the top and bottom and at the center marking. Do not push top and bottom pins all the way into the ball. Trim the eyelet at the bottom and top at a slight angle (B).

3 Position the center of 1 piece of red print ribbon just over the bound edge of the eyelet at the center marker, and pin. Bring the left edge of the ribbon to the outer edge of the eyelet binding at the top and bottom. Trim the right edge of the ribbon even with the inner bound edge of the eyelet (C). Holding the eyelet in place, remove the pins at the top and bottom and reinsert them through both the eyelet and the ribbon, pushing the pins all the way in.

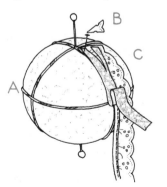

4 For the second row, position the eyelet on the ball with the bound edge next to the red print ribbon, so that the eyelet ruffle will overlap the ribbon. Pin and trim the ends as for the first piece of eyelet. Position and pin a green print ribbon in place as you did with the red print ribbon, continuing in the

eyelet-ribbon patterns and alternating ribbon colors until the ball is complete. You should have 16 rows of eyelet and 16 rows of ribbon.

5 As you apply the ribbon and eyelet, make sure the rows are parallel to the quarter markings. The ends of the eyelet should form a swirl at the top and bottom. Trim the ends of the eyelet as necessary so the swirls lie as flat as possible (D). Remove the large pins.

6 Make a hanging loop from green print ribbon and then finish it off with a bow of the same ribbon (see General Information, p. 56).

Ball C

1 Divide the ball into eighths (see General Information, p. 56).

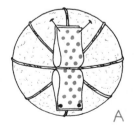

2 Cut 28 pieces of ⅝" (15mm) red print ribbon with edging, each 2" (5cm) long. Fold each piece of ribbon in half, wrong sides together and raw ends even, to form loops. (Edging is not shown in art.)

3 At the bottom of the ball, pin a loop on each side of the cross marker, centering the loops over one set of quarter markers; folds should meet at cross marker. Pin each raw corner in place (A).

4 Working from the bottom to the top on 1 quarter marker at a time, pin 7 loops on each quarter marker, each loop overlapping the one below by about ½" (13mm).

5 Cut 32 pieces of ⅜" (10mm) red print ribbon, each 1½" (3.8cm) long. Form loops. Starting at the bottom and working toward the top, pin 6 loops on each eighth marker, each loop overlapping the one below by about ⅜" (10mm). The 8 remaining loops will be used later.

6 Cut 40 pieces each of ⅜" (10mm) green ribbon and ½" (13mm) eyelet trim, all 1½" (3.8cm) long. Place the eyelet, wrong side down, over the right side of the ribbon and form loops (B).

7 Starting at the bottom and working toward the top, pin rows of 5 loops each in the remaining open spaces. Overlap the top 2 eyelet loops from

each row to cover the open space (C).

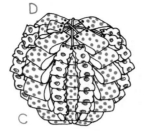

8 Pin the remaining red print ribbon loops at the top of the ball, placing 2 over each top pair of eyelet loops (D).

9 Make a hanging loop from green ribbon and eyelet trim, placing the eyelet right side up over the right side of the ribbon and tacking the layers together in several places. Attach the loop and finish off with a bow of eyelet trim (see General Information, p. 56).

Ball D

1 Divide the ball into eighths (see General Information, p. 56). Cut 32 pieces of ⅝" (15mm) green print ribbon with edging, each 2" (5cm) long. Fold each piece of ribbon in half, wrong sides together and raw edges even, to form loops. (Edging is not shown in art.)

2 Pin 8 loops to each quarter marker as done in Ball C, steps 3 and 4.

3 Cut 32 pieces of ⅜" (10mm) green ribbon, each 2" (5cm) long. Form these into "petals": holding the ribbon at its center point, fold up the right side, perpendicular to the left; then fold the left up over the right

so the raw edges meet (they won't align), forming a blunted diamond shape.

4 Starting at the bottom, pin 5 petals on each eighth marker, each petal overlapping the one below by about ⅜" (10mm) (A). The remaining 12 petals will be used later.

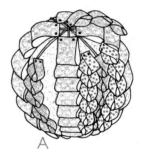

5 Cut 40 pieces of ⅜" (10mm) red print ribbon, each 2" (5cm) long. Form petals and pin these to the remaining open areas of the ball as in step 4, making 8 rows of 5 petals each. Overlap the top 2 red print petals from each row to cover the open space.

6 Use the remaining green petals to make 4 rows of 3 petals each above the last red petals (B), being careful to cover all open spaces.

7 Make a hanging loop from ⅜" (10mm) red print ribbon, and finish it off with a bow of the same ribbon (see General Information, p. 56).

Embroidered Felt Ornaments

Among the classiest you'll find anywhere, these 10 charming ornaments (illustrated in the color section following p. 48) are great take-along and finish-on-the-go crafts. Even novice embroiderers will find these a cinch to make, as they require only 5 embroidery stitches. If you prefer not to do the embroidery, use fabric paints instead. Spread the joy of these designs by reproducing them on different items of clothing for year-round use.

Finished size: approximately 3½″ × 5½″ (9cm × 14cm).

HOW-TO

1 Transfer ornaments (see Transferring Designs, p. 47) to white felt, transferring cutting lines for fronts, stitching lines, and motifs.

2 Embroider fronts, following the stitch and color key (see p. 148), using 4 strands of rayon floss or 3 strands of cotton floss. Cut out each embroidered front along the cutting line using pinking shears or regular shears. (Wreath only is shown in art.)

3 For a hanging loop, cut a 6″ (15cm) long piece of narrow braid, ribbon, or cording. Fold the loop in half and pin the ends to the back at the small •, so that the ends extend ½″ (13mm). Baste in place (A).

4 Center the wrong side of the embroidered front onto its contrasting back, matching stitching lines. Stitch along the stitching lines, through both

layers, leaving an opening for stuffing.

5 Stuff (see Stuffing, p. 44) lightly with fiberfill (B). Stitch the opening closed.

6 Apply gold cording or embroider over the stitching lines. To apply cording, center it over the stitching line, and butt the ends. Couch stitch in place (see Embroidery, p. 25) (C). For embroidery, use a chain stitch.

MATERIALS NEEDED

For 10 ornaments: (Note: yardage will change if fewer ornaments are made)

Ornament fronts
¼ yd (0.20m) of 72″ (180cm) white felt

Ornament backs
ten 7″ × 7″ (18cm × 18cm) contrast felt remnants

Trims and notions
2 yds (1.80m) of narrow braid, ribbon, or gold cording
4¼ yds (3.90m) of gold cording (optional)
13 skeins of embroidery floss: 1 skein each of yellow, light blue, dark green, hot pink, light purple, orange, dark purple, light green, red, dark blue, gold, pink, and burgundy
polyester fiberfill

Pattern pieces are found on pp. 146-149.

CUTTING INFORMATION

White felt: 1 front for each ornament
Contrast felt remnants: ornament backs, using either pinking shears or regular shears, cutting along cutting line for back

Victorian Ornaments

A touch of elegance and shimmering beauty can be yours with any of these 8 ornaments. Choose from among 3 styles of bell ornaments (decorated with lace, cord, or ribbon) and 3 styles of heart ornaments (also decorated with lace, ribbons—and dried flowers, too) for that delicate Old World touch. Or make the nosegay or strawberry to add a bit of springtime beauty to your Christmas tree. Make extra nosegays to tie onto your Christmas presents for that perfect finishing touch. These ornaments were made with remnants but you can use any fabric with a sheen to it, from polished cotton to lamés.

Finished sizes: bell A, B, or C—2⅜" high × 2¾" wide (6cm × 7cm); heart A, B, or C—2⅛" high × 2¼" wide (5cm × 5.5cm); strawberry—2¼" high × 2¼" wide (5.5cm × 5.5cm).

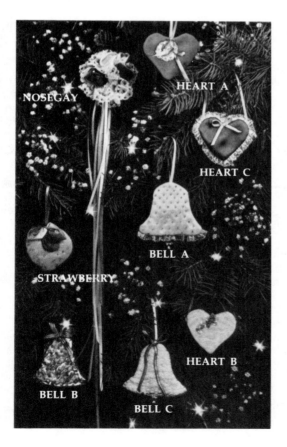

MATERIALS NEEDED

Bell A
4" × 8" (10cm × 20cm) fabric remnant
4" × 4" (10cm × 10cm) remnant of polyester batting
⅛ yd (0.20m) of ½" (13mm) lace ruffling
⅛ yd (0.20m) of ⅛" (3mm) ribbon
1 pkg small beads
1 small round bell

Bell B
4" × 8" (10cm × 20cm) fabric remnant
4" × 4" (10cm × 10cm) remnant of polyester batting
⅝ yd (0.60m) middy braid
1 pkg small beads

Bell C
4" × 8" (10cm × 20cm) fabric remnant
4" × 4" (10cm × 10cm) remnant of polyester batting
⅛ yd (0.20m) of ⅛" (3mm) ribbon
⅜ yd (0.40m) cord
½ yd (0.50m) of ½" (13mm) lace ruffling
1 small round bell

Heart A
3½" × 7" (9cm × 18cm) fabric remnant
3½" × 3½" (9cm × 9cm) remnant of polyester batting
⅛ yd (0.20m) of ½" (13mm) lace ruffling

¼ yd (0.30m) each of two ⅛″
  (3mm) contrast ribbons
1 skein ombré embroidery floss

Heart B

3½″ × 7″ (9cm × 18cm)
  fabric remnant
3½″ × 3½″ (9cm × 9cm)
  remnant of polyester batting
¾ yd (0.70m) each of three ⅛″
  (3mm) contrast ribbons

Heart C

3½″ × 7″ (9cm × 18cm) fabric
  remnant
3½″ × 3½″ (9cm × 9cm)
  remnant of polyester batting
¼ yd (0.30m) of ⅜″ (10mm) lace
  ruffling
⅜ yd (0.40m) each of two ⅛″
  (3mm) contrast ribbons
1 small bouquet of small dried
  flowers

Strawberry

¼ yd (0.30m) of 3″ (75mm)
  ribbon or 3½″ × 7″ (9cm ×
  18cm) fabric remnant
3½″ × 3½″ (9cm × 9cm)
  remnant of polyester batting
⅛ yd (0.20m) of 1″ (25mm)
  ribbon for leaves
⅛ yd (0.20m) of ⅛″ (3mm)
  ribbon
1 pkg small beads

Nosegay

½ yd (0.50m) of 1″ (25mm) lace
  ruffling
2½″ (6.5cm) of 1″ (25mm) ribbon
  for small leaves
1½″ (3.8cm) of 1½″ (38mm)
  ribbon for large leaf
⅛ yd (0.20m) of 1½″ (38mm)
  ribbon for flower
⅞ yd (0.80m) each of four ⅛″
  (3mm) contrast ribbons
1 yd (1.00m) of ⅛″ (3mm)
  contrast ribbon

**Pattern pieces are found on
p. 150.**

CUTTING INFORMATION

For 1 ornament

Fabric remnant: 2 bells *or* 2 hearts
Fabric remnant or ribbon: 2
  strawberries
Remnant of polyester batting: 1
  bell *or* 1 heart *or* 1 strawberry

HOW-TO

All seam allowances are ¼″ (6mm).

Bell A

1 To make the front, pin the batting to the wrong side of 1 fabric bell, basting along the seamline. Trim batting close to the basting (A).

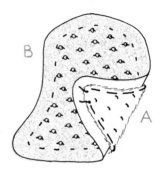

2 Sew the beads (see Beads, p. 16) to the front in a random pattern (B).

3 With right sides together, pin the front to the remaining bell section. Stitch, using a zipper foot, leaving an opening for turning. Trim and clip the seam.

4 Turn the bell right side out and press lightly. Slipstitch (see Hand Sewing, p. 34) the opening.

5 Pin the lace ruffling to the lower edge of the bell front, turning under the raw ends. Slipstitch it in place. Sew a small bell in the center of the lower edge (C).

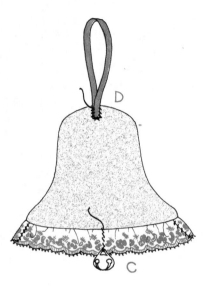

6 To make a hanging loop, fold 5″ (13cm) of ribbon in half. Sew it securely to the upper edge of the bell back (D).

Bell B

1 Prepare front as for Bell A, steps 1 through 4.

2 Cut 5″ (13cm) of middy braid. Fold it in half for a hanging loop, and sew it securely to the upper edge of the bell back.

3 Make a bow of the remaining middy braid and tack it in place at the upper edge of the bell front.

Bell C

1 Prepare the front as for Bell A, step 1.

2 Sew the first row of lace ruffling to the bell front, 1″ (25mm) up from the bottom edge, stitching along the bound edge of the lace.

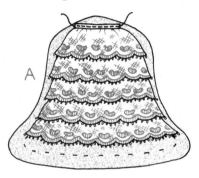

3 Stitch on 4 more rows of lace in the same manner, each row spaced ⅜″ (10mm) apart (A).

4 Stitch the sections, right sides together, as for Bell A, steps 3 and 4. Add the bottom row of lace, the small bell, and a ribbon hanging loop as you did for Bell A, steps 5 and 6.

5 Tie the cord into a bow and tack it to the upper front edge.

Heart A

1 To make the front, pin the batting to the wrong side of 1 fabric heart. Baste along the seamline. Trim the batting close to the basting.

2 For the center front "flower," embroider a series of bullion stitches (see Embroi-dery, p. 25) using 6 strands of floss. For the 3 inside stitches, wrap the needle 6, 9, and 12 times. For the 3 outside stitches, wrap the needle 15, 18, and 21 times.

3 Make a row of hand gathering stitches (see Gathering, p. 33) along the bound edge of the lace ruffling. Gather the lace, forming a circle around the stitches (A). Tack (see Hand Sewing, p. 34) the lace to the heart.

4 With right sides together, stitch the front to the remaining heart section, leaving an opening for turning. Trim and clip the seam.

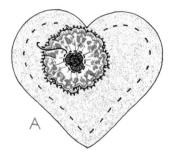

5 Turn the heart right side out and press lightly. Slipstitch (see Hand Sewing, p. 34) the opening.

6 To make a hanging loop, fold one ⅛″ (3mm) contrast ribbon in half. Sew it securely to the upper edge of the bell back.

7 Make a small bow using the other ⅛″ (3mm) contrast ribbon and tack it to the side of the flower (see photo).

Heart B

1 Prepare the front as for Heart A, step 1.

2 Using 1 color of ribbon, make flowers by embroidering 7 French knots (see Embroidery, p. 25), and following the design on the pattern. Using another color of ribbon, make petals by forming loops (A).

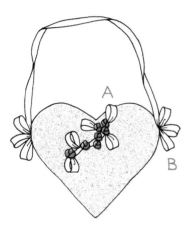

3 Complete as for Heart A, steps 4 and 5.

4 Fold 1 end of the remaining ribbon into 3 loops and tack to one side of the heart. Repeat for the other side of the heart, creating a hanging loop (B).

Heart C

1 Prepare as for Heart A, steps 1, 4, and 5.

2 Take one of the lengths of ribbon and form a small loop at one end and tack the loop to

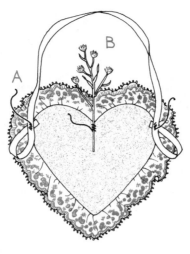

one side of the heart. Form a loop with the other end and tack it to the other side of the heart, creating a hanging loop (A). Tie the remaining piece of ribbon into a bow and tack it to the front of the heart.

3 Tack the lace ruffling around the outer edge of the heart. Tack a small bouquet of dried flowers to the back of the heart so the blossoms extend above the bow in front (B).

Strawberry

1 To make the front, pin the batting to the wrong side of the ribbon or fabric strawberry. Baste along the seamline. Trim the batting close to the basting.

2 Sew beads (see Beads, p. 16) to the front in a random pattern.

3 Pin the front to the remaining strawberry section, right sides together. Stitch, using a zipper foot, leaving an opening for turning. Trim and clip the seam.

4 Turn the strawberry right side out and press lightly. Slipstitch (see Hand Sewing, p. 34) the opening.

5 Make 3 leaves from the 1" (25mm) ribbon (see Gift Wrapping, page 129) and tack (see Hand Sewing, p. 34) to the top of the strawberry (see photo).

Nosegay

1 Gather by hand (see Gathering, p. 33) the bound edge of the lace ruffling, pulling up the gathers into a 3" (7.5cm) length. Fold the lace into thirds. Turn under the raw ends and hand sew in place (A).

2 Make 1 large leaf from the 1½" (38mm) ribbon, 2 small leaves from the 1" (25mm) ribbon, and 1 flower from the 1½" (38mm) ribbon (see Gift Wrapping, p. 129).

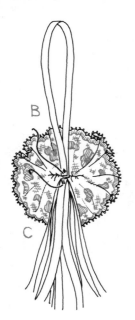

3 For a hanging loop, cut 5″ (13cm) from the 1 yd (1.34m) length of the ⅛″ (3mm) ribbon. Fold the ribbon in half and tack (see Hand Sewing, p. 34) the ends to the back of the nosegay (B). For streamers, fold the remaining 5 pieces of ⅛″ (3mm) ribbons in half. Tack the folds to the back of the nosegay (C). Trim the ends of the ribbons diagonally.

4 Hand sew the leaves and flower to the front of the nosegay (D).

Tree Skirt

This luxurious tree skirt is both beautiful and practical. It serves as a lovely backdrop for the gifts set under the tree while keeping your house tidy when those pine needles start to drop. Done here in the traditional red and green, the 6 wedges can each be done in a different color. Each wedge requires ¾ yd (0.70m) of 35" or 45" (90cm or 115cm) fabric. As you scan the pages of this book, think about using some of the shapes to appliqué on each wedge. Or make this an heirloom skirt by embroidering each family member's name and birth date on a different wedge.

Finished size: circumference approximately 150" (380cm).

MATERIALS NEEDED

Wedges, ruffle and extension (color 1)
3⅝ yds (3.40cm) of 35" or 45" (90cm or 115cm) fabric

Wedges (color 2)
2¼ yds (2.10m) of 35" or 45" (90cm or 115cm) fabric

Wedges (lining fabric)
2¼ yds (2.10m)

Trims and notions
⅝ yd (0.60m) of ¾" (20mm) self-gripping tape
8½ yds (7.80m) of 4" (100mm) flat eyelet
3 yds (2.80m) of ½" (13mm) eyelet beading with lace ruffling
3 yds (2.80m) of ¼" (6mm) ribbon or novelty trim for beading
5⅜ yds (5.00m) of ⅞" (22mm) ribbon

Pattern pieces are found on p. 151.

CUTTING INFORMATION

Fabric (color 1): 3 wedges; 6 ruffles; 1 extension
Fabric (color 2): 3 wedges
Lining: 6 wedges

Note: No pattern pieces are given for the ruffle or extension. Extension measures 21¼" × 3¼" (54cm × 8cm). Each ruffle measures 51" × 3½" (130cm × 9cm).

HOW-TO

All seam allowances are ⅝" (15mm).

1 Stitch the 6 fabric wedge sections together, alternating colors, and leaving 1 seam open. Weave ¼" (6mm) ribbon or trim through slits in the eyelet beading. Center and baste the eyelet beading over the seams on the right side. Stitch close to both long edges of the beading (A).

2 Stitch the short ends of the ruffle strips together, leaving 1 seam open, to form 1 long strip. Turn under ⅝" (15mm) on 1 long edge and both short ends, turning in ¼" (6mm) on raw edges and carefully folding in the fullness at the corners. Stitch in place and press. Machine gather (see Gathering, p. 33) the remaining raw edge of the ruffle.

3 With right sides together and seams and raw edges matching, pin the ruffle to the outer curved edge of the skirt, beginning and ending at the open edges, and with the short ends matching the seamlines. Adjust the gathers and baste (B).

4 Finish the short ends of the flat eyelet as you did on the ruffle. Machine gather the straight edge of the eyelet. Divide the eyelet into 6 equal sections, marking each section with a pin.

5 Pin the eyelet to the outer edge of the skirt, with the right side of the eyelet facing the wrong side of the ruffle. Match raw edges and ends of the eye-

let to the ends of the ruffle, and match pin markers to the wedge seams. Adjust the gathers and baste (C).

6 For the skirt back, stitch the 6 lining wedge sections together, leaving 1 seam open. Pin the back to the skirt, right sides together. Stitch, leaving one straight edge open. Trim the seam and clip the curves (D).

7 Turn the skirt right side out and press. Baste the raw open edges together.

8 Turn in ⅝" (15mm) on 1 long edge of the extension. Baste close to the fold and trim the seam allowance to ¼" (6mm).

9 Fold the extension in half lengthwise, right sides together, matching seamlines. Stitch the ends. Trim, turn to the right side, and press.

10 Pin the right side of the extension to the back, and stitch. Trim the seam, press toward the extension, and slipstitch (see Hand Sewing, p. 34) the basted edge over the seam (E).

11 Sew self-gripping tape to the opening edges of the skirt by hand or machine.

12 Make decorative bows (see Shirred Wreath, p. 71) and tack them to the outer edge of the skirt at each seam.

Decorating Your Home

Classic Christmas Stocking

What vision of Christmas is complete without stockings hanging from the fireplace mantel? Now you can make those classic old-fashioned Christmas stockings, complete with embroidered names, so everyone knows which one is meant just for them. They can be made in beautiful velvet, practical felt, or whatever fabric suits the person you're making it for. Don't just think of solid red and green when planning your collection of stockings; consider a lovely calico print bordered in a solid kettlecloth for anyone who loves Early American wares, or use denim to make a stocking for an active child. For a real "stocking" look, use candy-cane-striped fabric for the body of the stocking and a complementary solid for the heel, toe and band.

Finished size: 16" (40cm) long.

MATERIALS NEEDED

Stocking
½ yd (0.50m) of 35" or 45" (90cm or 115cm)
  fabric

Stocking band, heel and toe
½ yd (0.50m) of 35" or 45 " (90cm or 115cm)
  contrast fabric

Stocking lining
½ yd (0.50m) of 45" (115cm) lining fabric

Trims and Notions
⅞ yd (0.80m) of 1" (25mm) flat eyelet
1⅜ yds (1.30m) of ½" (13mm) eyelet beading
  with lace ruffling
1⅜ yds (1.30m) of ¼" (6mm) ribbon or novelty
  trim for beading
2½ yds (2.30m) of ⅞" (22mm) ribbon
remnant of embroidery floss
15" × 16" (38cm × 40cm) remnant of polyester
  batting

**Pattern pieces are found on
pp. 152-153.**

CUTTING INFORMATION

Fabric: 2 stockings
Contrast fabric: 4 stocking bands; 2 stocking
  heels; 2 stocking toes
Lining: 2 stocking linings
Polyester batting: 1 stocking lining

HOW-TO

All seam allowances are ⅝″ (15mm).

1 Staystitch (see Machine Stitching, p. 38) the inner curved edges of the heel and toe sections of each stocking. Pin 1 heel and 1 toe to each stocking, right sides together, clipping to the staystitching when necessary. Baste, then stitch the seams.

2 Insert ¼″ (6mm) ribbon or trim through the eyelet beading. On the right side of the stocking, pin the eyelet beading over the heel and toe seams. Stitch the beading close to both long edges.

3 With right sides together, stitch the stocking sections together, leaving the upper edge open (A). Trim the seams.

4 Trim the seam allowances from the batting. Pin the batting to the wrong side of the front stocking section. Catchstitch (see Hand Sewing, p. 34) the batting to the seams and the upper seamline (B).

5 Turn the stocking right side out and press gently. Stitch the lining sections, right sides together, leaving the upper edge open. Trim the seam. Slip the lining inside the stocking, *wrong* sides together. Baste the upper edge.

6 If desired, embroider a name (see Monograms, p. 183) on one band, transferring (see Transferring Designs, p. 47) and placing the lettering 1¼″ (3cm) below the foldline. Work

the letters in a chain stitch (see Embroidery, p. 25), using 3 strands of embroidery floss.

7 Stitch the embroidered band to one remaining band along a short unnotched end; press. Pin eyelet beading to the right side of the band, placing it 1″ (25mm) above the long unnotched edge. Stitch close to both long edges of the eyelet (C). Stitch remaining short edges of the band together.

8 Stitch the ends of the flat eyelet trim in a ¼″ (6mm) seam. Gather (see Gathering, p. 33) the eyelet by hand, ¼″ (6mm) from the raw edge. Pin the eyelet to the unnotched edge of the band, placing the gathering stitches along the band seamline. Adjust the gathers and baste. Turn in the seam allowance on the notched edge of the band. Baste and press (D).

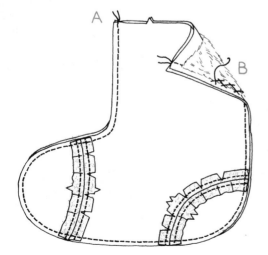

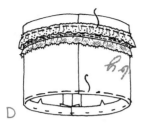

D

9 For the band facing, stitch the remaining band sections together along the short unnotched ends. Pin the facing to the band, right sides together, and stitch along the long unnotched edge. Trim the seam, turn the band right side out, and press.

10 Pin the notched edge of the band facing to the stocking, right sides together, with the embroidered side of the band matching the batting side of the stocking. Stitch (E). Press the seam toward the band.

11 Slipstitch (see Hand Sewing, p. 34) the basted edge of the band over the seam (F). Turn the upper edge of the band to the outside along the foldline. Press.

12 Make 2 bows from ⅞" (22cm) ribbon as for the Shirred Wreath (see p. 71), and tack the bows to the upper edge of the stocking, one at each seam.

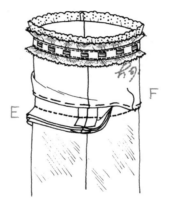

E   F

G

13 For a hanging loop, cut a piece of ⅞" (22cm) ribbon 14" (35.5cm) long. Turn in each end ½" (13mm). Baste and press.

14 Pin the ends of the ribbon, with turned-under ends facing the inside of the stocking at the upper edge of each seam. Sew the ribbon in place by hand (G).

Shirred Wreath

What better way to greet holiday guests than with a beautiful wreath of satin! Shown here in a 13" (33cm) diameter, and in a solid fabric, this wreath can also be quite eyecatching in a calico print. If your wreath will be exposed to the elements, consider making it in a lightweight ripstop nylon to maintain its beauty throughout many Christmas seasons.

Finished size: approximately 13" (33cm) in diameter.

MATERIALS NEEDED

Outer wreath and ruffle
1⅛ yds (1.10m) of 45" (115cm) fabric

Inner wreath
1 yd (1.00m) of 45" (115cm) lining

Trims and notions
3 yds (2.80m) of 4" (100mm) flat eyelet
2 yds (1.90m) of 1¾" (45mm) double edged eyelet
1⅜ yds (1.30m) of 2" (50mm) ribbon A
1⅜ yds (1.30m) of 1½" (38mm) ribbon B
1½ lbs (680 grams) of polyester fiberfill

No pattern pieces required.

CUTTING INFORMATION

Fabric: 3 outer wreaths, each 10" × 36" (25.5cm × 91.5cm); 3 ruffles, each 2½" × 36" (6.3cm × 91.5cm)

Lining: 1 inner wreath 9½" × 35½" (24cm × 90cm)

Double edged eyelet: 2 pieces, one 40" (101cm) and one 28" (71cm)

Ribbon A: 2 pieces, one 20" (51cm) and one 26" (66cm)

Ribbon B: 3 pieces, one 4" (10cm), one 18" (46cm), and one 24" (61cm)

Note: Inner wreath *must* be cut on the bias. To determine the bias grainline, cut the pattern piece from paper. Fold the upper left corner downward at a 45° angle so the lower edges meet. Crease the paper along the folded edge. Unfold and draw a line over the crease—the line is your bias grainline.

Shirred Wreath

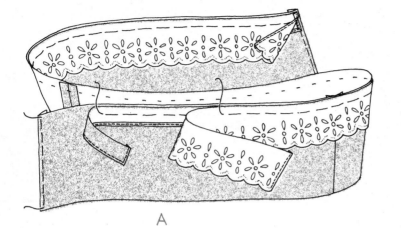

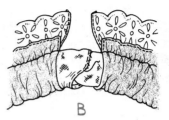

A

B

HOW-TO

All seam allowances are ⅝″ (15mm).

1 Fold the inner wreath in half lengthwise, and stitch the long edge. Turn in ⅝″ (15mm) on one open end. Baste and press.

2 Turn the inner wreath right side out. Hand gather (see Gathering, p. 33) the remaining end ⅝″ (15mm) from the raw edge. Pull up the gathering thread tightly to close the opening; stitch securely. Stuff firmly (see Stuffing, p.44) with fiberfill. Set aside.

3 Stitch the 3 outer wreath sections together along the short ends, leaving 1 end open to form a long strip. Stitch the 3 ruffle sections together along

the short ends, leaving 1 end open, to form a long strip. Press all seams open.

4 Turn in ⅝″ (15mm) on both short ends of the outer wreath. Baste and press.

5 Turn in both short ends and 1 long side of the ruffle ⅝″ (15mm). Then turn under the raw edges ¼″ (6mm), then ⅜″ (10mm), folding in the fullness at the corners; stitch and press.

6 Pin the ruffle to 1 long edge of the outer wreath. Baste.

7 Cut a piece of flat eyelet 105½″ (264cm) long. Finish the short ends as you did on the ruffle. Pin the eyelet to the outer wreath, right side of the eyelet facing the ruffle and with the finished ends even. Baste all 3 layers together (A).

8 Fold the outer wreath in half, lengthwise, right sides together, enclosing the ruffle and the eyelet. Stitch the long edges. Turn the wreath section right side out.

9 Slip the outer wreath over the stuffed inner wreath, arranging the shirring evenly. Bring the ends of the inner

C

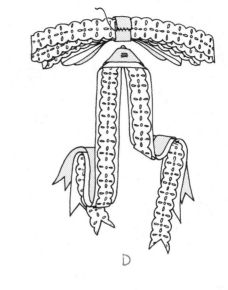

D

wreath together, lapping the open basted end ⅝″ (15mm) over the closed end. Slipstitch (see Hand Sewing, p. 34) in place (B).

10 Slipstitch the ends of the outer wreath, ruffle, and eyelet together.

11 For the bow, fold the 40″ (101cm) double edged eyelet into 2 loops, the larger one on the bottom. Then fold a 20″ (51cm) length of ribbon A into a single loop slightly smaller than the eyelet loops and place it on top of the eyelet. Finally, place an 18″ (46cm) length of ribbon B on top of that, smaller than ribbon A, and tack all the loops together in the center to form a four-looped bow.

12 Wrap a 4″ (10cm) length of ribbon B around the center of the bow, turning in ½″ (13mm) and lapping the raw end ½″ (13mm) on the back of the bow. Slipstitch the overlap closed (C).

13 Notch the ends of the remaining eyelet and ribbons. Placing ribbon A over the eyelet and ribbon B over ribbon A, tack all 3 together at the center point. Fold the eyelet and ribbons, with ribbon B on top, at a right angle to the tacked midpoint, to form a point. Tack the streamers to the back of the bow (D).

Nosegay Wreath

This charming wreath adds a touch of elegance to your Christmas decor and it can be made without much sewing at all. Lace, ribbon flowers and leaves combine for a beautiful and unique item you can make using small bits of time here and there. To complement your wreath, make 16 large nosegays and pin them to a 6" (15cm) styrofoam ball, add a touch of mistletoe, and you've got a kissing ball. Hang it in a well-traveled thoroughfare in your house and spread the joy of the season.

Finished Size: approximately 10" (25.5cm) in diameter.

MATERIALS NEEDED

5½ yds (5.10m) of 2" (50mm) craft ribbon for wreath

1⅝ yds (1.50m) of 1⅜" (35mm) craft ribbon for bow

1⅜ yds (1.30m) of 1" (25mm) ribbon for small flowers

¾ yd (0.70m) of 1½" (38mm) ribbon for medium flowers

¾ yd (0.70m) of 3½" (90mm) ribbon for large flowers

⅝ yd (0.60m) of 1" (25mm) ribbon for small leaves

1 yd (1.00m) of 1½" (38mm) ribbon for large leaves

2 yds (1.90m) of 1" (25mm) lace ruffling for small nosegays

3 yds (2.80m) of 1½" (38mm) lace ruffling for large nosegays

2¼ yds (2.10m) of ⅛" (3mm) ribbon for bows

⅞ yd (0.80m) each of five ⅛" (3mm) contrast ribbons

one 45" × 60" (115cm × 150cm) cribsize sheet of polyester batting

10" (25cm) Styrofoam ring

9 small round bells

No pattern pieces required.

74

HOW-TO

Nosegays

1 For the 6 small nosegays, cut 1″ (25mm) lace ruffling into six 12″ (30.5cm) strips. Gather (see Hand Sewing, p. 34) the bound edge of the lace and pull the gathers into a 3″ (7.5cm) length. Fold the lace into thirds. Turn under the raw ends and hand sew in place. Make 6 small leaves from 1¼″ (3.2cm) strips of 1″ (25mm) ribbon, and 6 large leaves (see Gift Wrapping, p. 129) from 1½″ (3.8cm) strips of 1½″ (38mm) ribbon. Make 6 small flowers (see Gift Wrapping, p.129) from 4″ (10cm) strips of 1″ (25mm) ribbon. Sew 1 small leaf, 1 large leaf, and 1 small flower inside each small nosegay.

2 For the 6 large nosegays, cut 1½″ (38mm) lace ruffling into six 18″ (46cm) strips. Gather the bound edge of the lace and pull the gathers into a 4½″ (11.5cm) length. Fold the lace into thirds. Turn under the raw ends and hand sew in place. Make 6 small leaves from 1¼″ (3.2cm) strips of 1″ (25mm) ribbon and 12 large leaves from 1½″ (3.8cm) strips of 1½″ (38mm) ribbon. Make 6 small flowers from 4″ (10cm) strips of 1″ (25mm) ribbon and 6 medium flowers from 4½″ (11.5cm) strips of 1½″ (38mm) ribbon. Sew 1 small leaf, 2 large leaves, 1 small flower, and 1 medium flower inside each large nosegay.

Wreath

1 Cut the batting into 3″ (7.5cm) wide strips. Wrap the batting around the wreath form, slightly overlapping the edges, until the wreath is about 8½″ (21.5cm) in circumference. Wrap the 2″ (50mm) craft ribbon over the batting, overlapping the edges slightly. Wrap the ribbon firmly but not tightly. Pin it in place at the ends (A).

2 Pin the nosegays around the wreath, alternating small and large ones, and leaving an open space on the wreath 5″ to 6″ (12.5cm to 15cm) long (B).

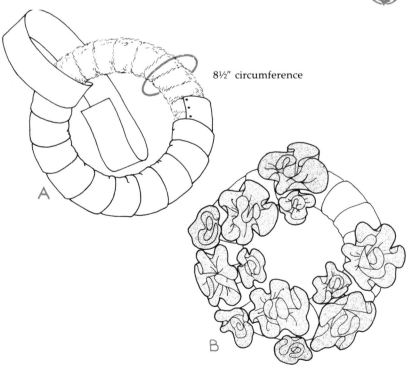

8½″ circumference

75

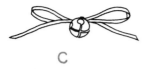

C

3 Cut the 2¼ yds (2.10m) of ⅛″ (3mm) ribbon into nine 9″ (23cm) pieces. Slip a bell onto each of the 9 strips and tie them into bows (C). Pin a bow to each large nosegay, and place the remaining 3 bows at random on the wreath (D).

4 For streamers, fold the 5 colors of ⅞ yd (0.80m) strips of ⅛″ (3mm) ribbon in half. Tack the folds onto the wreath near the end of the open area. Trim the ends of the ribbons diagonally.

5 Make 3 large flowers from 9″ (23cm) strips of 3½″ (90mm) ribbon, 6 large leaves from 1½″ (3.8cm) strips of 1½″ (38mm) ribbon, and 5 small leaves from 1¼″ (3.2cm) strips of 1″ (25mm) ribbon. Pin the 3 large flowers, 6 large leaves, and 5 small leaves to the wreath in the open space, covering the folded ends of the streamers (E).

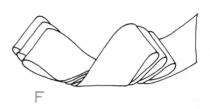

F

6 Fold the 1⅜″ (35mm) craft ribbon into several loops. Twist one side over the other, forming a loose bow (F), and tack (see Hand Sewing, p. 34) the bow through the center to the edge of the wreath, next to the large flowers (see photo).

7 For a hanger, secure a large safety pin to the back of the wreath, near the top.

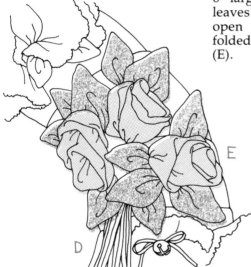

D

E

Fabric Basket

For an unusual Christmas centerpiece, make this lovely fabric basket for table or mantel. You can fill it with just about anything—home-baked Christmas cookies, dried flowers, or simply an arrangement of leftover Christmas ornaments. Use whatever fabric goes best with your decor: broadcloth, kettlecloth, linen, calico, or gingham. Enlarge it to make a casserole cosy or breadbasket, with or without the handle. You can use it year round if you wish, or make several in different seasonal colors—springlike pastels for Easter flowers, vivid summer shades for fresh fruit, warm autumn hues for an arrangement of everchanging fall foliage.

Finished size: 9" (23cm) in diameter.

MATERIALS NEEDED

Basket tubes, bottom and handle
⅞ yd (0.80m) of 45" (115cm) fabric A

Basket tubes
½ yd (0.50m) of 45" (115cm) contrast fabric B

Remnants and notions
10" × 10" (26cm × 26cm) remnant of polyester fleece
7 oz (200 grams) polyester fiberfill
11" × 15" (28cm × 38cm) red or white felt remnant for poinsettia
9" × 18" (23cm × 46cm) green felt remnant for leaves
2 medium pompoms

Pattern pieces are found on page 154.

CUTTING INFORMATION

Fabric A: 6 basket tubes; 2 bottoms; 1 handle 16¾" × 4¼" (42.5cm × 11cm)

Note: The handle *must* be cut on the bias. To determine the bias grainline, cut the pattern piece from paper. Fold the upper left corner downward at a 45° angle so the lower edges meet. Crease paper along the folded edge. Unfold and draw a line over the crease—the line is your bias grainline.

Fabric B: 5 basket tubes

Polyester fleece: 1 bottom

Red or white felt remnant: 2 poinsettia A; 2 poinsettia B

Green felt remnant: 2 poinsettia C

HOW-TO

All seam allowances are ⅝" (15mm).

1 Baste the fleece to the wrong side of 1 bottom section. Pin the remaining bottom section to this one, right sides together, and stitch, leaving an opening for turning. Trim and clip the seam.

2 Turn the bottom right side out and press. Slipstitch (see Hand Sewing, p. 34) the opening.

3 Fold each basket tube in half, lengthwise, right sides together. The short ends will not match evenly. Stitch the long edges, and trim the seam.

4 Turn each tube right side out, centering the seam in the back. Press lightly. Hand sew 1 end closed along the seamline, using a small running stitch (see Hand Sewing p. 34).

5 Using a long ruler or the eraser end of a pencil stuff (see Stuffing, p. 49) each tube with polyester fiberfill. Sew the remaining end closed along the seamline by hand, using a small running stitch (A).

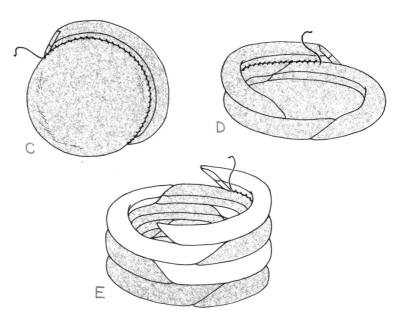

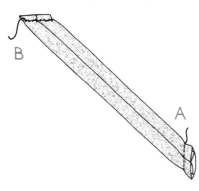

6 Turn in ⅝" (15mm) on each end, turning in ¼" (6mm) on the raw edges. Slipstitch the ends in place (B).

7 Pin 1 tube from fabric A to the outer edge of the basket bottom, turning the end of the tube under the basket bottom at the beginning and keeping the tube seam to the inside. Sew in place by hand (C).

8 Continue to pin and sew on the tubes, using 2 tubes of fabric A (D), then 2 tubes of fabric B, joining the tubes at the ends and keeping all tube seams to the inside (E).

9 Fold the handle in half lengthwise, right sides together, and stitch the long edge. Trim the seam.

10 Turn the handle right side out, bringing the seam to the center. Sew 1 end by hand along the seamline, using a running stitch.

11 Stuff the handle with polyester fiberfill. Sew the remaining end closed along the seamline, using a running stitch.

12 Sew the ends of the handle to the inside of the basket, turning in the ends ⅝" (15mm) and keeping the seam to the underside.

13 Make 2 poinsettias (see p. 84). Trim off most of the loop of the poinsettia. Hand sew the ends to the handle (see photo).

Santa Pillow

One look at Santa's lacy eyelet beard and you'll believe in him forever. Make a matching set for the holiday season, or make an extra front and appliqué it to a large piece of felt as a holiday wall hanging for a child's room.

Finished size: 21" high × 15½" wide (53cm × 40cm).

MATERIALS NEEDED

Pillow
½ yd (0.50m) of 45" (115cm fabric)

Hat A
⅜ yd (0.40m) of 45" (115cm) contrast fabric

Remnants
11" × 11" (28cm × 28cm) remnant of polyester batting
6½" × 10½" (17cm × 27cm) remnant 1 for face
5" × 7" (13cm × 18cm) remnant 2 for nose, mouth and cheeks
5" × 9" (13cm × 23cm) remnant 3 for eyebrows and mustache
2" × 2½" (5cm × 7cm) remnant 4 for eyes
11" × 14" (28cm × 36cm) remnant of fusible web

Trims and notions
5⅜ yds (5.00m) of 1¼" (32mm) eyelet ruffling
1 skein of 4-ply yarn
remnant of embroidery floss
1 lb (450 grams) of polyester fiberfill
2" × 5" (5cm × 13cm) piece of cardboard

**Pattern pieces are found on
pp. 155-156.**

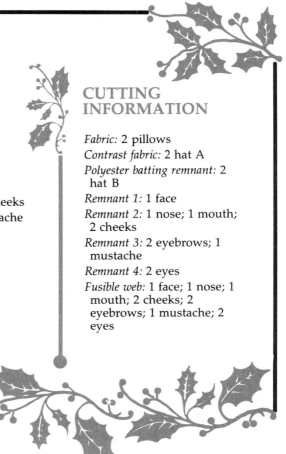

CUTTING INFORMATION

Fabric: 2 pillows
Contrast fabric: 2 hat A
Polyester batting remnant: 2 hat B
Remnant 1: 1 face
Remnant 2: 1 nose; 1 mouth; 2 cheeks
Remnant 3: 2 eyebrows; 1 mustache
Remnant 4: 2 eyes
Fusible web: 1 face; 1 nose; 1 mouth; 2 cheeks; 2 eyebrows; 1 mustache; 2 eyes

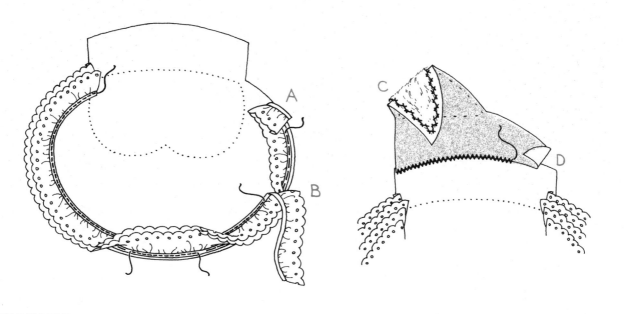

HOW-TO

All seam allowances are ⅜" (10mm).

1 For the front, pin a row of eyelet ruffling to one pillow section, right sides together, placing the bound edge of the eyelet ⅜" (10mm) inside the outer curved edge, ending at the placement line for the face. The ruffle edge will be pointing upward. Turn in ¼" (6mm) on both ends and baste the eyelet in place. Stitch the eyelet in place between the large ● 's (A).

2 Pin a second row of eyelet to the pillow front, having the bound edge 1" (25mm) inside the outer curved edge, with the ruffle edge pointing downward. Extend the raw ends ¼" (6mm) beyond the placement lines for face. Stitch along the bound edge of the eyelet (B). Apply 9 more rows of eyelet ruffling as you did for the second row, having each row ⅝" (15mm) above the previous stitching. All these rows of eyelet will have the ruffle pointing downward. To complete ruffling, cut 2 pieces of eyelet, each 2" (5cm) long. Center 1

piece ⅝" (15mm) above the last row you applied, curving it slightly. Pin and stitch as for the other rows. Center the second piece ⅝" (15mm) above the first and apply in the same manner.

3 Pin each hat B to the wrong side of each hat A section and catchstitch (see Hand Sewing, p. 34) to the seam allowances and the stitching line (C).

4 With the wrong side of the hat over the right side of the pillow, pin the hat sections to the front and back of the pil-

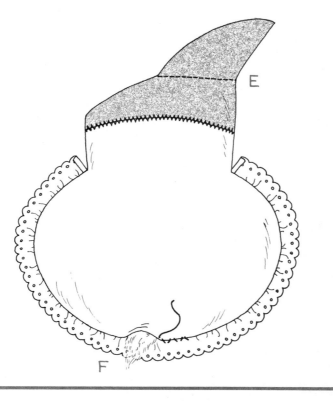

E

F

low, placing the lower raw edge of each hat ¼" (6mm) below the upper edge of each pillow. Machine zigzag each hat in place (D).

5 Fuse the appliqué pieces to the face, following manufacturer's directions for fusing, in the following order: eyebrows, eyes, cheeks, nose, mustache, and mouth. Machine zigzag (see Appliqués, p. 12) the raw edges of the appliqués in place, using a close zigzag stitch.

6 Work the satin stitch (see Embroidery, p. 25) on the eyes,

using 3 strands of embroidery floss.

7 Fuse the face to the pillow front, matching placement lines for the face, covering the raw ends of the eyelet trim and following manufacturer's directions for fusing. Zigzag the raw edges of the face in place.

8 Turning the lower ruffle away from the seamline, pin the pillow front to the back, right sides together. Stitch, leaving an opening between the large ● 's. The stitching should cover the bound edge

of the lower row of eyelet trim. Trim the seam, clip the corners, and turn the pillow to the right side. Press.

9 Stitch the hat along the stitching line (E). Stuff the pillow firmly with fiberfill (see Stuffing, p. 44) and slipstitch (see Hand Sewing, p. 34) the opening (F).

10 Make a yarn pompom (see Gift Wrapping, p. 129) and tack it to the top of the hat (see photo).

Holiday Appliquéd Apron

Get in the mood for baking Christmas goodies with this holiday apron. It's a snap to make in calico, broadcloth, muslin, or poplin. Don't limit yourself to the appliqués shown on these pages: create your own or choose one from any of the other projects in this book. Need a last minute gift when you're running short of time? Make the apron in any fabric and decorate it with iron-on decals.

Finished sizes: child's—center front 21⅜" (54cm); woman's: center front 26⅞" (68cm); man's—center front 31¼" (79cm).

MATERIALS NEEDED

Apron
1 yd (1.00m) of 45" (115cm) fabric for child's and woman's size
1⅛ yd (1.10m) of 45" (115cm) fabric for man's size

Tree
7" × 9" (18cm × 23cm) fabric remnant

Bow
3" × 3" (8cm × 8cm) fabric remnant

Notions
¾ yd (0.70m) of 20" (51cm) fusible web
1 pkg. wide bias tape to match apron (all sizes)

Pattern pieces are found on p. 157.

CUTTING INFORMATION

Fabric: 1 apron; 3 strips, each 1½" (3.8cm) wide and 45" (115cm) long. Cut across fabric from selvage to selvage.
Remnants: 1 tree; 1 bow
Fusible web: 1 tree; 1 bow
Wide bias tape: two 12" (30.5cm) strips for child's size *or* two 14" (35.5cm) strips for woman's size *or* two 17" (43cm) strips for man's size

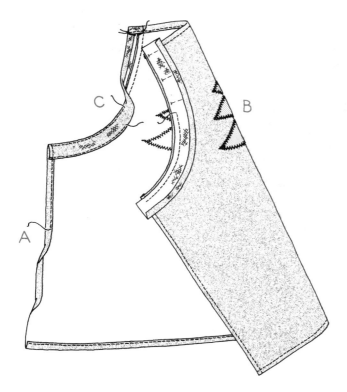

HOW-TO

All seam allowances are ¼" (6mm).

1 Position the tree at the center of the apron, having the top of the tree 6" (15cm) below the top edge of the apron. Fuse in place following manufacturer's directions for fusing. Position the bow at the top of the tree and fuse in place. Machine zigzag (see Appliqués, p. 12) the raw edges.

2 Hem the straight sides, top, and bottom by turning in ½" (13mm), then turning the raw edge under ¼" (6mm). Stitch in place (A).

3 To form the casings, unfold one edge of the wide bias tape and pin it to the right side of the apron along the curved edges, matching raw edges and extending the ends of the bias tape ¼" (6mm) beyond the finished edges of the apron. Stitch in a ¼" (6mm) seam (B).

4 Turn under the ends of the bias tape to make them even with the apron edges. Stitch the ends. Turn the bias to the inside along the seamline, forming a casing. Stitch close to both long edges of the bias through all thicknesses (C).

5 To make the tie, stitch the 1½" (3.8cm) fabric strips together in ¼" (6mm) seams to form one long strip. Fold the strip in half lengthwise, right sides together. Stitch the long edge in a ¼" (6mm) seam.

6 Turn the tie right side out and press. Insert the tie through the casing, using a bodkin, leaving enough of the tie at the top to form a loop to drape around the neck. Knot the ends of the tie.

Christmas Table Decorations:

FABRIC TREE, TABLE RUNNER, PLACEMATS, NAPKINS, NAPKIN RINGS, AND POINSETTIAS

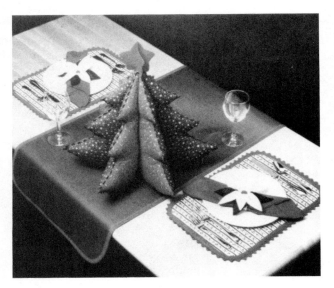

Add a colonial American flavor during the holiday season with these functional table decorations. They are simple to make in an evening or two, and you can choose from a variety of fabrics: broadcloth, kettlecloth, linen, or calico. Make them for your own home or as a thoughtful gift. Consider appliquéing any of the other Christmas shapes in this book on the placemats, table runner, or napkins. Or decorate the placemats with lace or rickrack around the edge to use all year round.

Finished sizes: tree—20″ (51cm) tall; table runner—20½″ wide × 54″ long (52cm × 140cm); placemat—11⅜″ × 17″ (29cm × 43cm); napkin—22″ (56cm) square; poinsettia—7¾″ (19.5cm) in diameter.

HOW-TO
All seam allowances are ⅝″ (15mm).

Tree

1 Pin the rickrack to each fabric A tree section, centering the rickrack on the seamlines and tapering the ends into the seam allowance at the small • 's at the bottom of each section (A). Baste.

2 Pin 1 contrast fabric B tree to each fabric A tree, right sides together. Stitch, leaving an opening between the small • 's. Clip inward corners, trim

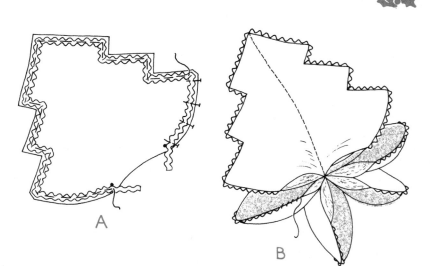

MATERIALS NEEDED

Tree

¾ yd (0.70m) of 45" (115cm) fabric A

¾ yd (0.70m) of 45" (115cm) contrast fabric B

6¾ yds (6.20m) jumbo rickrack 9" × 9" (23cm × 23cm) red felt remnant for star

4½" × 9" (11.5cm × 23cm) remnant of fusible web

30 oz (900 grams) polyester fiberfill

Table runner

1⅝ yds (1.50m) of 45" or 60" (115cm or 150cm) fabric

1⅝ yds (1.50cm) of 45" (115cm) polyester fleece

4¼ yds (3.90m) of ½" (13mm) double fold bias tape

Placemats (to make 2)

¾ yd (0.70m) of 45" or 60" (115cm or 150cm) fabric

⅜ yd (0.40m) of 45" (115cm) polyester fleece

3⅛ yds (2.90m) of ½" (13mm) double fold bias tape

3⅛ yds (2.90m) of jumbo rickrack

Napkins (to make 2)

¾ yd (0.70m) of 45" or 60" (115cm or 150cm) fabric

Poinsettias (to make 2)

11" × 15" (28cm × 38cm) red or white felt remnant

9" × 18" (23cm × 46cm) green felt remnant

2 medium pompoms

Pattern pieces are found on pp. 158-159.

CUTTING INFORMATION

Tree: Fabric A—3 trees; contrast fabric B—3 trees

Star: Remnant of red felt—4 stars; remnant of fusible web—2 stars

Table runner: Fabric—2 rectangles, each 20½" × 54" (52cm × 137cm); polyester fleece—1 rectangle 20½" × 54" (52cm × 137cm)

Placemats: Fabric—4 rectangles, each 11⅜" × 17" (29cm × 43cm); polyester fleece—2 rectangles, each 11⅜" × 17" (29cm × 43cm)

Napkins: Fabric—2 squares, each 22" × 22" (56cm × 56cm)

Poinsettias: White or red felt remnant—2 poinsettia A, 2 poinsettia C; green felt remnant—2 poinsettia B

---

straight across outer corners, and trim and clip all seams.

3 Turn the tree sections right side out. Turn in the seam allowances on the open edges. Baste and press. Do not close the openings.

4 Mark the center of each tree section. Pin all 3 sections to-gether, matching the centers, placing the first two sections with fabric B sides together, and the third section matching fabric A sections. Baste. Stitch along the center line, through all thicknesses.

5 Using a long ruler or the eraser end of a pencil, stuff (see Stuffing, p. 44) the tree sections firmly with fiberfill. Slipstitch (see Hand Sewing, p. 34) the openings (B).

6 For the treetop star, sand-wich each piece of fusible web between 2 squares of felt, wrong sides together, and fuse, following manufacturer's directions for fusing (C).

7 Transfer (see Transferring Designs, p. 47) the star pattern to each felt square. Edgestitch (see Machine Stitching, p. 38) all edges of each star and cut them out (D).

8 Pin the 2 star sections together, matching stitching lines. Stitch through all layers (E).

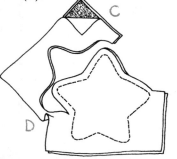

9 Sew the star to the top of the tree (see photo).

Table Runner and Placemats

1 Round off all corners on the fabric and fleece rectangles using the corner guide on p. 158. Note: Placemats only are shown in art.

2 Pin the fleece to the wrong side of 1 fabric section (A). Pin the wrong side of the remaining fabric section over the fleece and baste the raw edges together (B).

3 Encase the raw edges with double fold bias tape (see Bias Binding, p. 19). Stitch close to the inner edges of the tape, through all layers (C), turning under and overlapping the raw end of the tape. Slipstitch (see Hand Sewing, p. 34) in place.

4 For the placemats, pin rickrack to the bias tape, centering it on the outer edge of the tape and turning under one end and lapping the remaining raw end of the rickrack. Baste. Stitch (D).

Napkins

1 Turn in ⅜" (10mm) on all edges, turning under the raw edge ¼" (6mm). Press. Stitch close to the inner edges of the hem.

Poinsettias

1 Stitch sections A and B along stitching lines in the middle of each section (A). Slash between the stitching.

2 Bring the lines of small • 's together on sections A, B, and C to make the tucks. Stitch between the small • 's (B).

3 Place section A over section B, matching slashed sections. Insert the pointed ends of C through the slashes from the section B side. Tack (see Hand Sewing, p. 34) the pompom to the middle of the flower (see photo) (C).

A

B

Napkin Rings

1 For each napkin ring, make one poinsettia as above.
2 Slip the rolled or folded napkin through the loop on the wrong side of the poinsettia.

C

Santa Christmas Card Holder

Here's a fun way to display your Christmas cards: in the pouch of a smiling Santa wall hanging! Do it entirely by machine appliqué—out of calico, broadcloth, muslin, chintz, or polished cotton. Santa's jolly face can also decorate many other holiday items, from table linens to aprons, for a festive touch.

Finished size: 16" × 24¾" (41cm × 63cm).

88

CUTTING INFORMATION

Fabric A: 1 front, a 16½" × 26½" (42cm × 67cm) rectangle; 2 bag linings, each 13¾" × 11½" (35cm × 29cm) rectangles
Fabric B: 1 back, a 16½" × 26½" (42cm × 67cm) rectangle; 2 cheeks; 1 heart; 1 hat; 1 jacket
Remnant 1: 2 bags
Remnant 2: 1 beard; 2 cuffs; 1 circle; 2 eyebrows
Remnant 3: 2 eyes
Fleece: 1 hat; 1 jacket; 1 beard
Fusible web: 2 cheeks; 1 heart; 2 eyebrows; 2 cuffs; 1 circle; 2 eyes

HOW-TO

All seam allowances are ¼" (6mm).

1 Round off the corners along one 13¾" (35cm) edge of the bag and bag lining sections, using the corner guide on p. 160.

2 On the right side of the front, draw 1 placement line, 9" (23cm) long, 11¾" (30cm) up from 1 short edge and 3¾" (9.5cm) in from each long side.

3 Fuse 2 cuffs and 1 circle to the jacket along the placement lines, following manufacturer's directions for fusing. Baste the fleece to the wrong side of the jacket. Pin the fleece side of the jacket to the front, placing the lower edge of the jacket along the placement line you drew.

4 Cut away the face section from the beard along the cutting lines. Baste the beard fleece to the wrong side of the beard fabric, and pin the beard to the front of the jacket and along the beard placement line, fleece side down.

5 Pin and fuse the cheeks, eyebrows, and eyes to the front in the face area, following the photo on p. 88 for placement. Unpin and remove the beard.

6 Baste the jacket to the front, close to the raw edges of the jacket. Baste the fleece to the wrong side of the hat and, using the beard to determine placement, baste the hat to the front, fleece side down, close to its raw edges (A). Baste the beard in place.

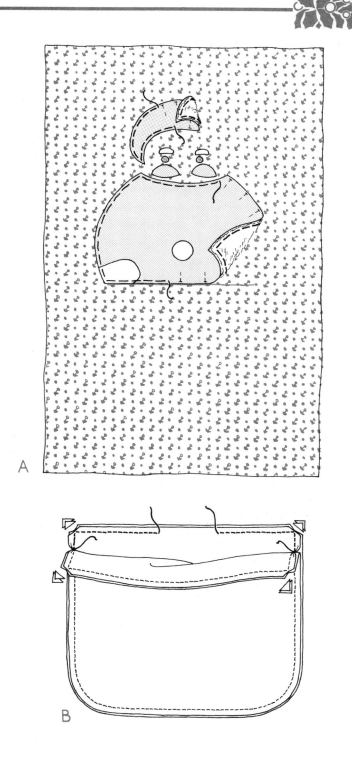

A

B

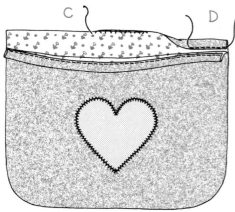

7 Zigzag all edges and stitching lines (see Appliqué, p. 12), except the lower edge of the jacket.

8 Fuse the heart to the right side of 1 bag piece, centering the heart 3″ (7.5cm) up from the curved lower edge. Zigzag the heart edges.

9 With right sides together, stitch the 2 bag sections together, beginning and ending stitching 1¼″ (3.2cm) from the upper edge. Turn the bag right side out.

10 Stitch the bag lining sections together as for the bag. Slip the lining over the bag, right sides together, and stitch the upper edges, breaking the stitching at the previous stitching, and leaving a 4″ (10cm) opening on the middle of 1 edge. Trim the corners diagonally (B).

11 Turn the bag right side out through the opening in the lining. Slip the lining into the bag

and slipstitch (see Hand Sewing, p. 34) the opening (C).

12 Fold ⅝″ (15mm) of each upper edge to the inside to form a casing. Press and stitch close to the seamed edge (D).

13 Cut the ribbon in half. Insert 1 piece through each casing. Center the bag over the front, placing the casing stitching line ¼″ (6mm) up from the placement line you drew on the front. Stitch the bag to the front on the casing stitching, only along the width of the jacket. Pivot and stitch up across the casing at either side of the jacket (E). Trim the rib-

bon ends diagonally and pull the ribbons up, forming gathers. Tie the ends into bows (F).

14 Pin the back to the front, right sides together. Stitch, leaving an opening along the upper edge for turning. Turn right side out, press, and slipstitch the opening.

15 Fold 1″ (25mm) to the back along the top edge. Stitch close to the lower edge, forming a casing for the dowel rod. To hang, slip the dowel into the casing and tie a length of cord securely on the ends of the dowel.

90

Gifts and Gift Wrapping

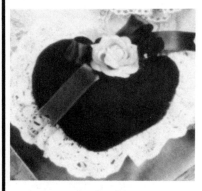

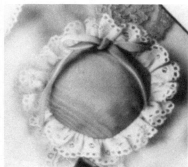

Sachets

These pretty, delicately scented little sachets can be made in different shapes—heart, butterfly, or round—for yourself or as a gift. Experiment with a variety of fabrics— piqué, satin, moiré, broadcloth, chintz—and decorate them with different laces and ribbons.

Finished sizes: heart sachet—5" (12.5cm) high; round sachet—3⅝" (9cm) in diameter; butterfly sachet—5" (12.5cm) high.

MATERIALS NEEDED

Heart sachet

7" × 14" (18cm × 36cm) fabric remnant

1¼ yds (1.20m) of 1" (25mm) flat lace

⅜ yd (0.40m) of ½" (13mm) ribbon for bow

1 purchased flower *or* ⅛ yd (0.20m) of 1½" (38mm) ribbon for 1 medium ribbon rose

1 oz (30 grams) sachet

Round sachet

7" × 14" (18cm × 36cm) fabric remnant

1 yd (1.00m) of 1½" (38mm) eyelet

½ yd (0.50m) of ¼" (6mm) ribbon

1 oz (30 grams) sachet

Butterfly sachet

7" × 14" (18cm × 36cm) fabric remnant

¾ yd (0.70m) of ⅜" (10mm) edging

½ yd (0.50m) of ¼" (6mm) ribbon

1 oz (30 grams) sachet

Pattern pieces are found on pp. 162-163.

CUTTING INFORMATION

Fabric remnant: 2 heart sachets *or* 2 butterfly sachets *or* 2 round sachets

HOW-TO

All seam allowances are ⅝" (15mm).

1 *For the heart and the round sachets*, stitch the ends of the eyelet or flat lace together in a ⅝" (15mm) seam to form a continuous loop. Stitch again ¼" (6mm) away from the first stitching in the seam allowance. Trim close to the stitching and press the seam to one side (A).

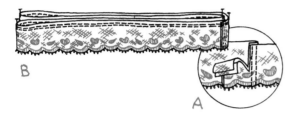

2 Make 1 row of gathering stitches (see Gathering, p. 33) ⅝" (15mm) from the raw edge and another row ⅜" (10mm) from the raw edge. Fold the trim into quarters, marking the divisions with pins (B).

3 Divide the heart or round sachet into 4 equal sections and mark with pins. Match the pin markers on the trim to the pin markers on the sachet section, right sides together, placing the lower row of gathering stitches along the seamline. Adjust the gathers to fit and baste in place (C).

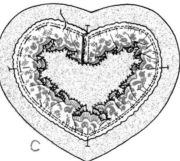

4 *For the butterfly*, place the straight side of the edging over the seamline of 1 sachet section, turning under and lapping 1 end of the edging ¼" (6mm) over the other end. Baste in place (D).

5 *For all 3 sachets*, stitch the remaining sections to the trimmed sections, right sides together, leaving an opening for turning. Trim the seams. On the heart and the butterfly, clip the seam at the inner corners.

6 Turn right side out. Fill with sachet and slipstitch (see Hand Sewing, p. 34) the opening. For the heart and round sachets, notch the ends of the ribbon and tie into a bow. Tack (see Hand Sewing, p. 34) the bow to the inner corner of the heart and near an edge of the round. If desired, make 1 medium ribbon rose (see Gift Wrapping, p. 129). Tack the purchased flower or the ribbon rose over the bow on the heart.

7 *For the butterfly*, trim the ends of the ribbon diagonally. Wrap the ribbon around the sachet and tie it into a bow near the top (see photo).

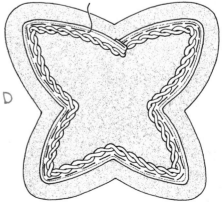

Cosmetic Case

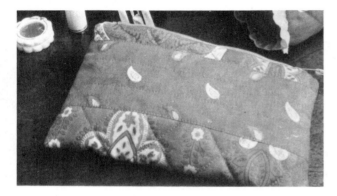

Almost everyone will welcome a new cosmetic case for Christmas, and they'll never guess how easy this one is to make! You can quilt your own fabric in calico, broadcloth, poplin, chintz, or satin, or use prequilted fabric when time is short. One of the contrasting bands can be embroidered with a name or initials to set off this case. Reduce the size by half and you've got a handy change purse to match.

Finished size: 8" × 4½" (20cm × 11.5cm).

MATERIALS NEEDED

Note: Cosmetic case can be made from prequilted fabric or you can quilt your own fabric.

If using prequilted fabric

10" × 12" (26cm × 31cm) piece of prequilted fabric remnant for case (fabric A)

10" × 7" (26cm × 18cm) contrasting fabric for band (fabric B)

10" × 12" (26cm × 31cm) plastic remnant for lining

⅜ yd (0.40m) of ⅜" (10mm) grosgrain ribbon

7" (18cm) zipper

If quilting your own fabric

10" × 12" (26cm × 31cm) fabric remnant for case (fabric A)

10" × 18" (26cm × 46cm) contrasting fabric remnant for quilt backing and band (fabric B)

10" × 12" (26cm × 31cm) plastic remnant for lining

10" × 12" (26cm × 31cm) polyester batting remnant for quilting

⅜ yd (0.40m) of ⅜" (10mm) grosgrain ribbon

7" (18cm) zipper

No pattern pieces required.

CUTTING INFORMATION

For prequilted fabric

Fabric A: one 8½" × 9¾" (22cm × 25cm) rectangle for case

Fabric B: two 8½" × 3" (22cm × 7.5cm) rectangles for bands

Lining: one 8½" × 9¾" (22cm × 25cm) rectangle

For self-quilted fabric

Note: Self quilting must be done before cutting (see Quilting, p. 40).

Fabric A: one 8½" × 9¾" (22cm × 25cm) rectangle for case

Fabric B: one 8½" × 9¾" (22cm × 25cm) rectangle for backing; two 8½" × 3" (22cm × 7.5cm) rectangles for bands

Polyester batting remnant: one 8½" × 9¾" (22cm × 25cm) rectangle

Lining: one 8½" × 9¾" (22cm × 25cm) rectangle

HOW-TO
All seam allowances are ⅝" (15mm).

1 Machine quilt your fabric unless you are using prequilted fabric (see Quilting, p. 40).

2 Turn under the long edges of each band ¼" (6mm). Press. Pin the wrong side of each band to the right side of the case, placing each band 1" (25mm) in from each short edge. Stitch close to both long pressed edges of the bands and again ¾" (20mm) in from each pressed edge (A).

3 Fold the bag in half, right sides together, so the bands are facing each other. Place the zipper, face down, to each side of the case so that the right side of the zipper faces the right side of the fabric and the edges of the zipper are even with the raw edges. Position the zipper stop ¾" (20mm) in from the long edge and pin in place. Turn back the tops of the zipper tape. Baste the tape in place. Stitch close to the zipper teeth, using a zipper foot (B).

4 Open the zipper. Pin the side seams, right sides together, and stitch (C). Turn right side out, turning in any remaining seam allowances at the upper edge.

5 Fold the plastic lining in half, matching short ends, and stitch the short sides. Turn down ⅜" (10mm) along both upper edges.

6 Slip the lining into the case, wrong sides together, and slipstitch (see Hand Sewing, p. 34) it to the zipper tape, having all raw edges between the case and the lining.

7 Make a zipper pull from ribbon (see Ribbons, p. 42).

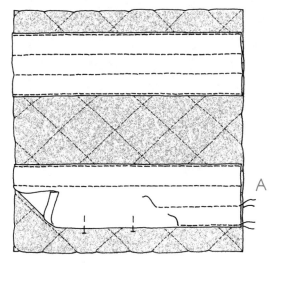

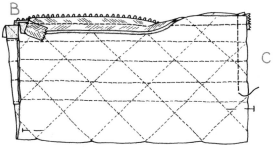

Quilted Tote

You can make this great carryall for weekends, shopping trips, or overnight visits in 3 sizes. It's a snap to make because it uses double-faced prequilted fabric. Turn your tote into a picnic basket by adding a lining of batting-backing plastic and you're ready for a day at the park.

Finished sizes: small bag—11" (28cm); medium bag—13" (33cm); large bag—20" (50cm).

MATERIALS NEEDED

Small bag

⅞ yd (0.80m) of 35" or 45" (90cm or 115cm) double-faced prequilted fabric

12" (30cm) zipper

1 pkg ½" (13mm) double fold bias tape

Medium bag

1¼ yd (1.20m) of 35" or 45" (90cm or 115cm) double-faced prequilted fabric

14" (35cm) zipper

1 pkg ½" (13mm) double fold bias tape

Large bag

1⅝ yd (1.50m) of 35" (90cm) or 1⅜ yd (1.30m) of 45" (115cm) double-faced prequilted fabric

20" (50cm) zipper

1 pkg ½" (13mm) double fold bias tape

Pattern pieces are found on pp. 164-165.

CUTTING INFORMATION

Small, medium, or large bag

Double-faced prequilted fabric: 1 bag; 2 sides; 2 straps; 2 tabs

HOW-TO

All seam allowances are ⅝" (15mm).

1 Reinforce the long sides of the bag through the ■ 's and large ● 's. Stitch along the seamline, using small machine stitches.

2 Turn in both of the long edges of each strap ⅝" (15mm). Press. Fold each strap, right sides together, matching the folded edges. Stitch across the short ends. Trim the seams.

3 Turn the straps right side out. Baste close to the pressed edges. Edgestitch close to both long edges and topstitch ¼"

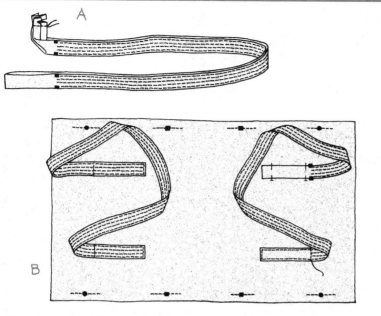

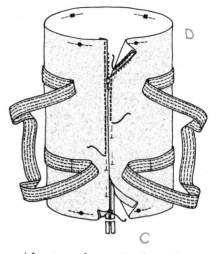

(6mm) away from the long edges, between the symbols (A).

4 Pin the straps to the bag, matching the symbols. Stitch close to the outer edges of the strap ends and again ¼" (6mm) away from the edges, meeting the previous stitching lines (B).

5 Turn in the seam allowances on both short sides of the bag. Press. Center the closed zipper, face up, under the opening edges, with the pull tab ¾" (20mm) in from one end, pin. Since the bottom of the zipper will extend beyond the edge, whipstitch (see Hand Sewing, p. 34) across the teeth, ⅝" (15mm) in from the edge of the bag. Trim off the excess zipper ½" (13mm) below the new zipper stop. With a zipper foot, stitch the zipper in place (C).

6 On the inside, trim the seam allowances even with the zip-

per tape. Overcast (see Hand Sewing, p. 34) the seam allowance and zipper tape together (D).

7 Stitch the tab sections, right sides together, leaving the end opposite the point open. Trim the seam and trim across the corners, turn right side out and press. Baste the raw edges together. Topstitch the tab ¼" (6mm) from the finished edges. Pin the tab to the bag along the end with the new zipper stop, matching raw edges and having the point of the tab at the center of the zipper. Baste the tab to the bag ⅝" (15mm) from the raw edge.

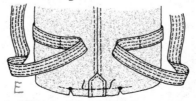

8 Clip the bag to the reinforced ■'s and ●'s (E). With right

sides together, pin the sides to the bag, matching the symbols at the corners. Stitch, pivoting at each symbol (F). Trim the seams to ¼" (6mm).

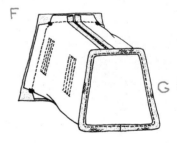

9 Encase the raw edges of the seams with double fold bias tape, turning in at the ends (see Bias Binding, p. 19) to meet at the lower edge (G). Or zigzag the raw edges to clean finish them.

10 Cut a 6" (15cm) piece of double fold bias tape. Stitch close to the long open edges and trim the ends diagonally. Insert the tape in the zipper pull and tie it into a knot.

Tie, Cummerbund, and Ascot

A special gift for the special man in your life. Use satin, brocade, linen, taffeta, or twill for the tie and cummerbund and luscious crepe de chine, tissue faille, or silk jacquard for the ascot. If you're making yourself a dressy outfit for a special holiday party, why not buy a little extra fabric and make the man in your life a tie to match? And don't limit these lavish gifts to the men on your list. By shortening the back elastic on the cummerbund you can fit it to a woman's waist.

Finished sizes: tie—2½" (6.3cm) wide; cummerbund—5½" (14cm) wide; ascot—42" (106cm) long.

MATERIALS NEEDED

Tie

⅞ yd (0.80m) of 35", 45" or 60" (90cm, 115cm, or 150cm) fabric

¼ yd (0.30m) of 45" (115cm) lining fabric

⅞ yd (0.80m) of 36" or 45" (90cm or 115cm) interfacing

Cummerbund

½ yd (0.50m) of 35", 45", or 60" (90cm, 115cm, or 150cm) fabric

1 yd (1.00m) of 45" (115cm) lining

½ yd (0.50m) of 36" (90cm) non-woven interfacing

½ yd (0.50m) of 1½" (38mm) elastic

one 1½" (38mm) interlocking buckle

two 1½" (38mm) adjustable sliders

Ascot

1⅜ yds (1.30m) of 35", 45", or 60" (90cm, 115cm, or 150cm) fabric

Pattern pieces are found on pp. 166-167.

CUTTING INFORMATION

Tie

Fabric: 1 tie A; 1 tie B

Lining: 1 tie facing A; 1 tie facing B

Interfacing: 2 interfacing A; 1 interfacing B; 2 interfacing C

Cummerbund

Fabric: 1 cummerbund; 2 cummerbund sides

Lining: 1 cummerbund lining

Interfacing: 1 cummerbund; 2 cummerbund sides

Ascot

Fabric: 1 ascot

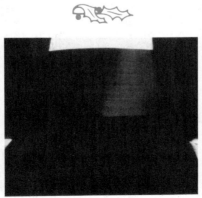

HOW-TO

All seam allowances are ⅝" (15mm).

Tie

1 Stitch the tie A and B sections, right sides together, at the notched end. Press seam open. Fold each end of the tie in half, right sides together, matching the raw edges. Stitch across the ends from the fold to the small •. Trim, and press the seam open with the point of your iron (A).

2 Pin tie facing A and tie facing B to the tie ends having raw edges even. Stitch each pointed end beginning at the small • and stitching outward. Trim seam close to stitching (B).

3 Fold the pointed ends of each tip up ¼" (6mm), forming a roll line, matching symbols. Stitch the side edges, pivoting across the seam allowance at the symbols. Clip diagonally to the symbols and trim the seam (C).

4 Turn the facings to the inside along the roll lines and side seams. Press lightly. Baste the side edges in place.

5 Baste interfacing A sections together through the centers. Baste interfacing B to A, matching centers and the lower straight edges. Hand sew through the centers (D).

6 Sew interfacing C sections together securely by hand

through the centers. Lap the notched ends of interfacing A and C, matching seamlines. Stitch. Trim close to the stitching (E).

7 Pin the interfacing to the left edge of the tie, placing the center of the interfacing along the left seamline of the tie, matching symbols (F). Stitch along the seamline securely by hand.

8 Turn in the seam allowance on the remaining long edge of the tie. Baste (G). Turn the long edges to the back of the tie along the roll lines, lapping the turned-under edge over the interfaced edge and matching seamlines. Slipstitch (see Hand Sewing, p. 34) between the symbols (H). Press lightly.

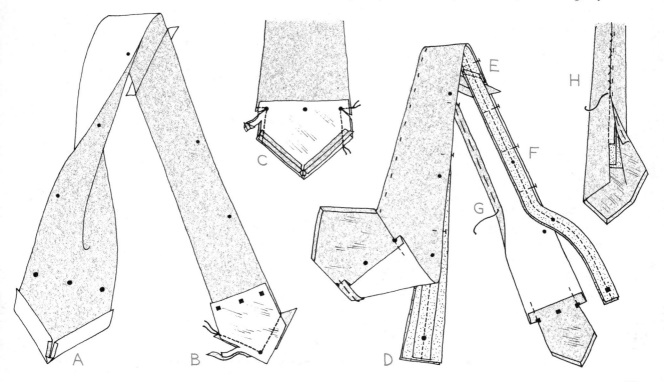

Cummerbund

1 Baste the interfacing to the wrong side of the cummerbund. Sew invisibly by hand along the foldlines (A).

2 Make pleats on the outside as indicated on the pattern. Baste.

3 Baste interfacing to the wrong side of each cummerbund side section. Stitch the side sections to the front. Trim the interfacing close to the stitching (B).

4 Cut the elastic into two 9" (23cm) pieces. Slip 1 end of an elastic piece through the middle bar of a slide adjuster, extending the end ¾" (20mm). Baste, then stitch the end in place (C). Repeat with the other elastic and slide adjuster.

5 Slip the remaining end of the elastic over the bar end of the buckle section, threading the elastic back through the slide adjuster (D). Repeat with the other elastic and buckle.

6 Pin each section of the elastic to each end of the side, with the buckle facing the pleats (E). Baste. Pin the lining to the cummerbund, right sides together. Stitch, leaving an opening for turning. Trim the seams.

7 Turn the cummerbund right side out through the opening. Slipstitch (see Hand Sewing, p. 34) the opening and press.

Ascot

1 Fold the ascot in half lengthwise, right sides together. Stitch the raw edges together beginning at the pointed ends and leaving an opening on the long side for turning.

2 Trim the seams and turn the ascot right side out. Press. Slipstitch (see Hand Sewing, p. 34) the opening.

3 Crease along the lines of small • 's to make pleats. Bring the creases to the lines of large ● 's. Baste. Stitch along the stitching lines, as shown (A). Press.

Needleworker's Carryall Tote

*Every needleworker's delight, this organized bag can carry
knitting, needlepoint, and embroidery projects. It's divided inside
with loops to hold yarns, needles, and scissors. You can make this
handy tote in a variety of fabrics including piqué, broadcloth,
chintz, and canvas. No needleworkers in the family? Then replace
the loops, needle holder, and scissors pocket with one or more
interior pockets and you've got an all-purpose tote that doubles as
a soft-sided briefcase. To show off your handiwork, embroider a
monogram on the outside.*

Finished size: 14¼″ × 16¼″ (36cm × 41cm).

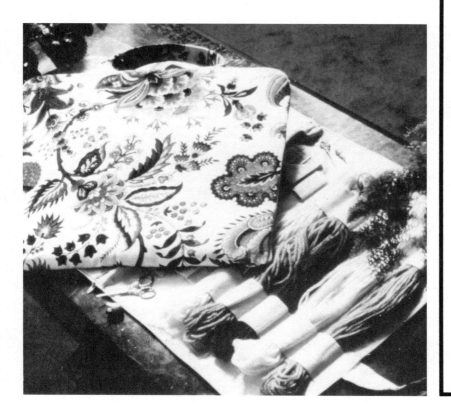

MATERIALS NEEDED

⅞ yd (0.80m) of 45″ (115cm)
  fabric
⅞ yd (0.80m) of 45″ (115cm)
  lining
⅞ yd (0.80m) of 25″ (64cm)
  non-woven interfacing
2½″ × 3″ (7cm × 8cm) felt
  remnant
two 22″ (55cm) zippers

**Pattern pieces are found on
pp. 168-169.**

CUTTING INFORMATION

Fabric: 1 bag; 2 handles
Lining: 1 bag; 1 pocket; 2
  loops; 1 scissors pocket; 1
  needle holder
Interfacing: 1 bag
Felt remnant: one 1⅞″ × 2⅝″
  (4.8cm × 6.7cm) rectangle

HOW-TO

All seam alowances are ⅝" (15mm).

1 Baste the interfacing to the wrong side of the bag fabric. Fold each handle in half lengthwise, with right sides together. Stitch the long edges. Trim the seam, turn right side out, and press. Baste the handles to each short side of the bag, matching symbols and raw edges (A).

2 Open the zippers and center the zipper stops at the center of each long side of the bag, placing the zippers face down. Pin the zipper tapes along the edges with the teeth extending beyond the seamlines, toward the center of the bag. Taper the top ends of the zipper tape into the seam allowances. Baste, then stitch the zippers in place using a zipper foot (B).

3 Turn the upper edge of the pocket 1½" (3.8cm) to the wrong side, turning the raw edge in ¼" (6mm). Stitch and press. Make pleats on the right side of the pocket as indicated on the pattern, bringing the pleat lines together. Baste the pleats in place and across the upper and lower edges (C).

4 Turn in ⅝" (15mm) on the lower raw edge of the pocket. Baste close to the fold. Trim the basted seam allowance to ¼" (6mm). Now, position the wrong side of the pocket to the right side of the bag lining along the placement lines. Baste the sides in place and stitch close to the lower edge of the pocket.

5 Fold the loop sections in half lengthwise, right sides together. Stitch the long edges. Trim the seams, pressing the seams open with the point of your iron. Turn the loop sections right side out, centering the seams, and press. Baste the ends of the loops to the bag lining on the opposite short side, matching symbols. Stitch along the stitching lines closest to the low edge, as shown (D).

6 Match the stitching lines on the loops to those on the bag lining and stitch, forming small loops (E).

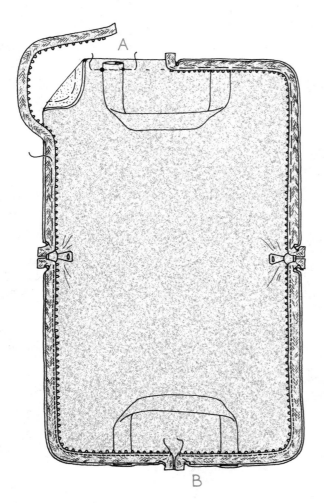

7 Fold the scissors pocket in half crosswise. Stitch the raw edges, leaving an opening for turning. Trim the seam, turn right side out, and slipstitch (see Hand Sewing, p. 34) the opening. Press. Pin the pocket on the bag lining over the raw end of the left-hand row of loops, at the placement lines, with the folded edge toward the middle of the bag. Stitch close to the edges of the pocket, leaving the folded edge open (F).

8 Fold the needle holder in half crosswise, right sides together, and stitch, leaving an opening for turning. Trim the seam, turn right side out, and press. Slipstitch the opening.

9 Center the felt between the placement lines on the needle holder. Stitch close to all edges of the felt. Pin the needle holder, with the felt face up, to the bag lining, above the right-hand row of loops, matching the stitching lines on the needle holder to the placement lines on the bag lining. Stitch along the stitching lines on the needle holder. Fold the remaining side of the holder over the felt side and press (G).

10 With right sides together, pin the lining to the bag. Stitch, leaving an opening for turning. Trim the seam, being careful not to cut into the zipper tape. Turn the bag right side out and press. Slipstitch the opening.

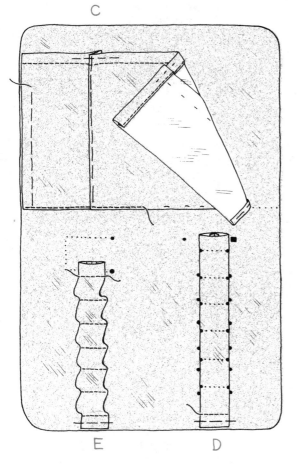

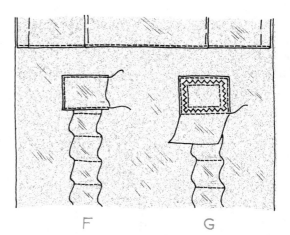

103

Drawstring Gift Bag

As useful as it is lovely, this lined drawstring bag is perfect for that hard-to-wrap gift, and the receiver will remember your thoughtfulness each time it is used. A wide variety of fabrics are suitable, from functional broadcloth to lightweight handkerchief linen to more luxurious satin and peau de soie. Double the dimensions of the bag and you quadruple its uses: a handy laundry bag in canvas, a roomy beach tote in duck, or a child's all-purpose bag in denim; add a new toy occasionally and watch the delight in the children's eyes as they open the drawstring.

Finished size: approximately 10″ × 12″ (25.5cm × 30.5cm).

MATERIALS NEEDED

⅞ yd (0.80m) of 35″ or 45″ (90cm or 115cm) fabric for bag and lining
1¾ yds (1.60m) of ³⁄₁₆″ (5mm) cording
1½ yds (1.40m) of 1¼″ (32mm) double-edged flat lace
2½ yds (2.10m) of 1¼″ (32mm) single-edged flat lace

No pattern pieces required.

CUTTING INFORMATION

Fabric: four 11¼″ × 13¼″ (29cm × 34cm) rectangles for bag and bag lining
Note: Round off 2 corners on one 11¼″ (29cm) side of each bag and bag lining piece, using corner guide on p. 170.

HOW-TO

1 On the right side of 2 bag sections, pin and stitch 2 strips of double-edged flat lace, each strip centered on a line 3″ (7.5cm) in from each long side.

2 Cut a piece of single-edged lace 55″ (140cm) long. Make 2 rows of hand gathering (see Gathering, p. 33) stitches along the straight edge of the lace, the first row close to the edge and the next row ¼″ (6mm) away. Pull up the gathers and pin the lace to the sides and lower curved edge of 1 bag section, placing the straight edge ⅜″ (10mm) in from the raw edges. Taper the lace ends into the seam allowance at a point 3⅜″ (8.5cm) down from the upper edge. Baste the lace in place (A).

3 Pin the 2 lace-trimmed bag sections, right sides together, and stitch the long sides and lower curved edge, leaving a ½″ (13mm) opening 2⅞″ (7.3cm) down from the upper edges on both sides of the bag.

4 Turn the bag right side out and press lightly. With each end extending ⅝″ (15mm), pin the remainder of the single-edged lace around the top of the bag on the outside, matching the straight edge of the lace to the raw edge of the bag. Trim off the excess, leaving two extended ⅝″ (15mm) ends. Unpin the ends and sew them wrong sides together ½″ (13mm) in from the ends. Trim the ends close to the stitching.

B

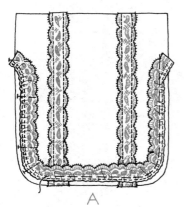

A

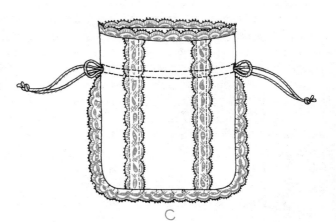

C

Bring the right sides of the lace together, making a crease along the seam. Press and stitch ⅛" (6mm) from the seam, enclosing the raw edges. Press the seam to one side (B). Repin the lace to the bag and baste the lace in place.

5 Stitch the remaining bag sections, right sides together, for the lining, leaving a 2" (5cm) opening at the center of the lower edge. Trim the seam.

6 Slip the bag inside the lining, right sides together, matching upper raw edges. Pin and stitch the upper edges. Trim the seam. Pull the bag out through the opening in the lining and press lightly. Slipstitch (see Hand Sewing, p. 34) the lining opening.

7 Turn the lining down inside the bag. On the outside, make 2 rows of stitching to form a casing, 1 row 2¼" (5.6cm) and the other 2¾" (7cm) down from the upper edge, aligned with the ½" (13mm) opening.

8 Cut the cording in half. Using a bodkin or safety pin on

1 end, slip the cording through 1 side opening, bringing the end around the bag and out the same side opening. Knot the ends together. Insert the other piece of cording through the other side of the bag in the same manner. Knot the ends (C).

Cap'n Joshua Teddy Bear

What childhood is complete without a teddy bear to love, cuddle, and share secrets with? This large bear is a fully dressed smiling sailor and captain of the Happiness Crew, and all the more lovable because you made it yourself. Use short-pile fabric for an authentic furlike feel and set off the paws with remnants of either velveteen, suede, or flannel. Use sailor-blue fabric for the clothing or any color that your child will like. Why not turn Cap'n Joshua into Cap'n Jill? Make a skirt from an 8" × 20" (21cm × 51cm) piece of fabric. Seam the short ends, narrow hem the bottom, make a casing for elastic at the top, and you're all set!

Finished size: 20" (51cm).

Cap'n Joshua Bear is a member of the S.S. Happiness crew. Both are trademarks of Determined Productions, Inc.

MATERIALS NEEDED

Bear
½ yd (0.50m) of 60" (150cm) short-pile fabric
8" × 8" (21cm × 21cm) remnant for paws and soles

Jacket and pants
⅝ yd (0.60m) of 45" (115cm) fabric

Hat
⅜ yd (0.40m) of 45" (115cm) fabric
14" × 20" (36cm × 51cm) remnant for band and brim

Trims and notions
1¾ yds (1.60m) of ⅜" (10mm) gold trim
⅜ yd (0.40m) of 18" or 22" (46cm or 56cm) heavy weight fusible interfacing
polyester fiberfill
black tapestry yarn
four ⅝" (15mm) buttons and snap fasteners

Pattern pieces are found on pp. 171-173.

HOW-TO

All seam allowances are ¼" (6mm). Note: for sewing with fake fur see Fabrics, p. 30.

1 Stitch the neck darts on the head side pieces. Press the darts flat. For each ear, stitch 2 ear sections, right sides together, along the curved edge, leaving the straight edge open. Trim the seam, turn right side out, and baste the raw edges together. Using small stitches, stitch ¼" (6mm) from all lower raw edges through the small • 's. Clip to the small • 's. Pin the ears to the head sides, matching the small • 's and large ● 's. Baste in place (A).

2 Pin the upper head darts together, matching raw edges and enclosing the ears. Stitch. Press the darts toward the back of the head (B).

3 Pin the head side sections to the head front, right sides together, matching large ● 's, small • 's, and ■ 's. Clip the head sides as needed to sew the seam. Stitch from the large ● at the nose to the ■ at the back of the head. Stitch the head side sections together below the nose, ending at the large ● (C).

4 Pin and stitch the body front sections, right sides together, along the center front seam from the neck edge to the ■ 's, matching notches. Pin and stitch the inner curved edge of each foot section to the body leg front, easing it in place (D).

5 Fold the tail in half, right sides together, matching small • 's. Stitch the outer curved edge. Trim the seam, turn right sides out, and stuff (see Stuffing, p. 44) lightly with fiberfill. Baste the raw edges together. Baste the tail to one body back section, with the seam pointing downward, matching symbols and raw edges on the center back seamline (E).

6 Pin and stitch the body back sections together along the center back seam between the large ● and ■, catching the tail. Leave the seam open above the large ● and below the ■. Pin and stitch the body front to the body back at the shoulders and sides, matching notches and

CUTTING INFORMATION

Note: When cutting fake fur or high-pile fabrics, cut only one layer of fabric at a time. Where there are 2 pattern pieces to be cut from the same pattern piece, make sure you cut 1 with the pattern right side up, and the other with the pattern right side down.

Pile fabric: 2 head sides; 1 head front; 2 body fronts; 2 body backs; 2 upper arms; 2 under arms; 2 feet; 4 ears; 1 tail

8" × 8" (21cm × 21cm) remnant: 2 paws; 2 soles

Jacket and pants fabric: 2 jacket fronts; 1 jacket back; 2 jacket sleeves; 2 jacket collars; 2 pants

Hat fabric: 1 hat; 1 hat facing

14" × 20" (36cm × 51cm) remnant: 1 hat band; 2 hat brims

Interfacing: 1 hat; 1 hat band; 1 hat brim; 1 hat facing

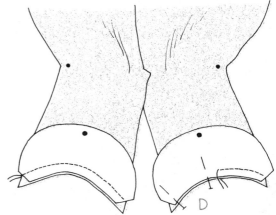

A

B

C

D

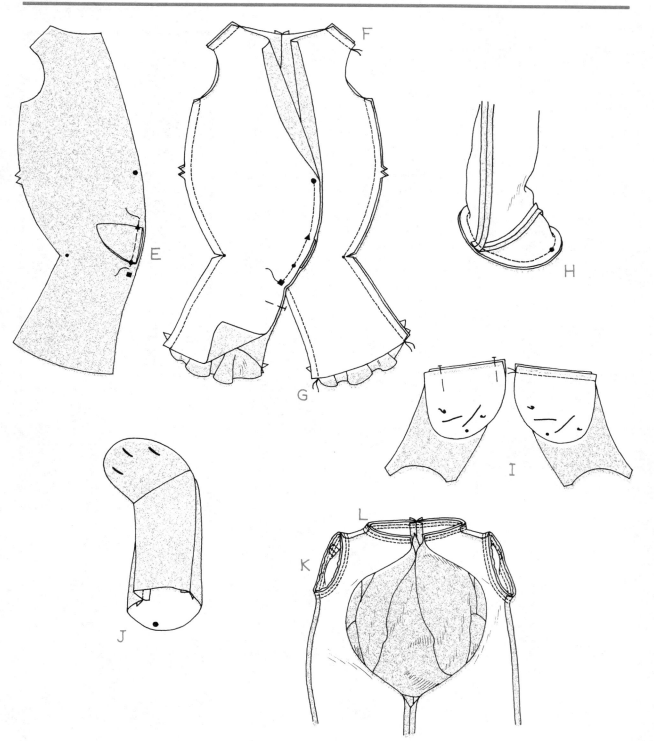

small • 's. Clip to the small • 's (F). Stitch the inner leg seams, ending at the ■ (G).

7 Embroider the soles along the stitching lines, using a straight stitch (see Embroidery, p. 25). Pin and stitch the soles to the foot and leg back, right sides together, matching the large ● 's (H).

8 Embroider each paw along the stitching lines, using a straight stitch. Pin and stitch the paws to the under arms, right sides together, along the straight edges (I). Pin and stitch the upper arms to the under arms, right sides together, matching small • 's, and leaving the shoulder edge open. Trim the seam and turn the arm right side out (J).

9 Pin one arm in the armhole so it is inside the body, right sides together, and matching raw edges. Match the large ● to the shoulder seam. Adjust the ease and stitch (K). Stitch

again, ⅛″ (3mm) away in the seam allowance. Repeat with the other arm.

10 Pin the head, right sides together, into the body, as you did with the arms, matching the raw edges with the neck. Pin at the neck seam and match the head side darts to the shoulder seams. Stitch (L).

11 Turn the bear right side out. Stuff firmly with fiberfill, using small handfuls and pushing the stuffing into the arms and legs with a ruler or the eraser end of a pencil. Slipstitch (see Hand Sewing, p. 34) the center back opening.

12 Using 4 strands of black tapestry yarn, embroider the mouth and eyebrows with stem stitches (see Embroidery, p. 25), and the nose and eyes with satin stitches, following the stitching lines (M).

Jacket

1 Turn under ⅛″ (3mm) along the straight edge of the jacket front self facing. Stitch. Stitch

along the seamline on both sides of the inner corner of the front at the self facing foldline, using small stitches. Clip the front to the stitching. Stitch the front to the back at the shoulder seams.

2 Stitch the collar sections, right sides together, along the outer edge. Trim the seam, trimming between the stitching lines (N). Turn the collar right side out and press.

3 Pin the collar to the right side of the jacket, placing the small • 's at the shoulder seams. Baste in place. Turn the self facing to the outside, along the foldline. Pin. Stitch the entire neck seam (O). Stitch the lower edge of the jacket, across the facing, ⅜″ (10mm) up from the lower edge, ending at the large ●. Trim the seams (P).

4 Turn the facing to the inside and press. On the right side of the jacket, stitch through all thicknesses close to the neck seam, keeping the collar free.

5 Turn up the lower edge of each sleeve ⅜″ (10mm) to the

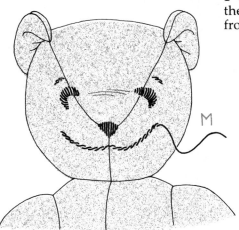

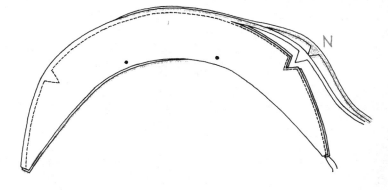

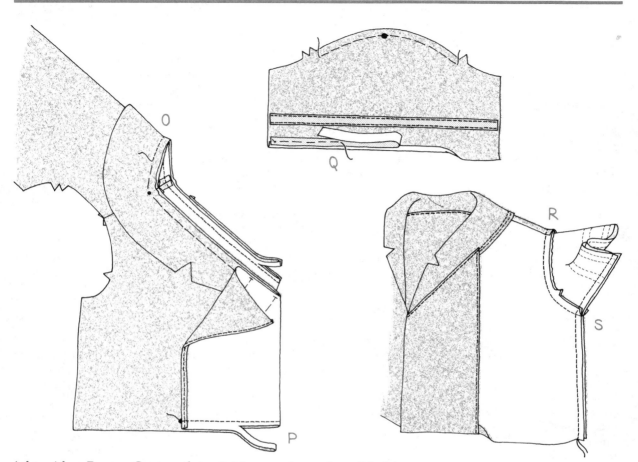

right side. Press. Center the gold trim over the placement line and turned-up raw edge. Baste, then stitch close to both long sides of each piece of trim (Q).

6 Pin each sleeve to the jacket armhole, right sides together, matching large • 's to the shoulder seams and matching notches. Ease to fit, and stitch the sleeve in place (R).

7 Pin the back to the front at the sides, matching sleeve seams. Stitch each sleeve and side in a continuous seam (S).

8 Narrow hem (see Machine Stitches, p. 38) the remaining lower edge of the jacket, turning it up ³⁄₈″ (10mm) and turning in ¼″ (6mm) on the raw edge. Press and stitch.

9 Sew the buttons to the right side of the left front at the markings. Sew the snaps on the inside.

Pants

1 Center and pin gold trim to each pant section, centering it over the placement line. Stitch close to both long edges of the trim.

2 With right sides together and matching notches, stitch each inner leg seam (T).

3 Turn one pant leg right side out and slip it into the other leg so the right sides are together. Pin along the crotch seam. Stitch, leaving an opening between the small • 's for the bear's tail (U).

4 Press the crotch seam open. Stitch close to the pressed edges of the opening (V).

5 Narrow hem the upper and lower edges of the pants. Turn

110

hem ⅜″ (10mm) to the wrong
side, turning in ¼″ (6mm) on
the raw edge. Press and stitch.

Hat

1 Fuse the interfacing to the
wrong side of the hat band following manufacturer's directions for fusing. Fold the band
lengthwise, wrong sides together, and press. Baste the
raw edges together. Center the
gold trim over the placement
line, turning in ¼″ (6mm) on
the raw ends. Baste. Stitch
close to both long edges of the
trim and across the ends (W).

2 Fuse interfacing to the wrong
side of one hat brim section.
With right sides together, pin
the remaining brim section to
the interfaced one and stitch
along the outer curved edge.
Trim the seam and turn right
side out. Baste the raw edges
together.

3 Pin the brim to the un-
trimmed side of the band along
the folded edge, matching the
small •'s and the center line.
Stitch close to the folded edge
of the band (X).

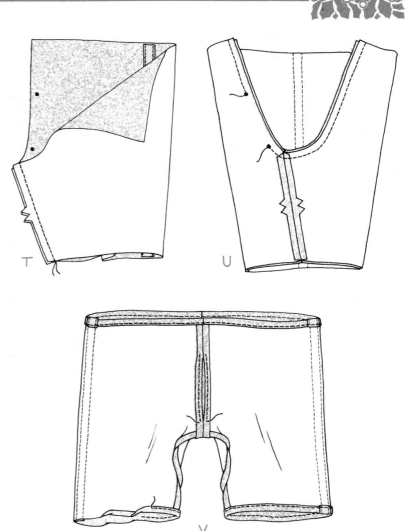

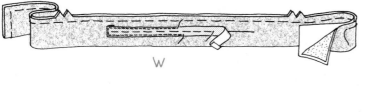

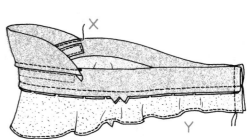

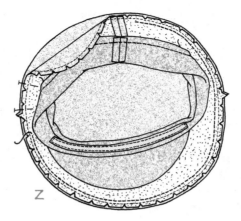

4 Fuse interfacing to the wrong side of the hat facing. Staystitch both curved edges of the facing ⅛" (3mm) from the seamline in the seam allowance. Pin the inner curved edge of the facing to the band, right sides together opposite the brim, matching notches and centers, and clip the facing to the staystitching as needed. Stitch. Press the seam toward the facing.

5 Stitch the center back seam of the band and facing in one continuous seam (Y).

6 Fuse the interfacing to the wrong side of the hat. Pin the hat to the facing, right sides together, matching notches and clipping the facing to the staystitching as needed. Stitch (Z). Turn the hat right side out.

Sleeping Baby, Carrier, and Coverlet

This precious sleeping baby doll comes with its own special coverlet and carrier. The 12" (30.5cm) doll is made in a stretchable knit, and single-faced prequilted fabrics are used for the coverlet and carrier. You can line the carrier and coverlet with any remnants of calico, broadcloth, muslin or gingham—but be careful to avoid diagonal, plaid, or striped fabric. A gift like this will bring a smile to a child's face on any gift-giving occasion, not just Christmas.

Finished sizes: doll—12" (30.5cm); carrier—17" long × 11" high (43cm × 28cm); coverlet—12" (30.5cm) square.

MATERIALS NEEDED

Doll

20" × 20" (51cm × 51cm) stretchable knit remnant

Carrier and coverlet

¾ yd (0.70m) of 45" (115cm) prequilted fabric

⅝ yd (0.60m) of 45" (115cm) contrast fabric for lining

Trims and notions

3⅜ yds (3.10m) of 1¼" (32mm) flat lace

1½ yds (1.40m) of ⅜" (10mm) flat lace

3⅞ yds (3.60m) of ⅜" (10mm) ribbon

light brown and pink embroidery floss

6 oz (180 grams) polyester fiberfill

½ yd (0.50m) curly yarn

Heavy-duty thread

Powder blush

Pattern pieces are found on pp. 174-175.

CUTTING INFORMATION

Stretchable knit: 2 doll bodies; 2 doll arms

Prequilted fabric: 1 carrier side; 1 hood; 1 carrier bottom; two 21½" × 2¾" (54.5cm × 7cm) rectangles for straps; one 13" (33cm) square for coverlet

Contrast fabric: 1 carrier side; 1 carrier side band; 1 hood band; 1 hood; 1 carrier bottom; one 13" (33cm) square for coverlet lining

HOW-TO

All seam allowances are ¼" (6mm).

Doll

1 Pin 1¼" (32mm) flat lace to each arm, placing the bound edge of the lace over the placement line. Stitch (A).

2 Fold each arm in half, right sides together, and stitch, leaving the upper edge open. Turn right side out and stuff (see Stuffing, p. 44) with fiberfill. Baste the upper raw edges together.

3 Pin two pieces of 1¼" (32mm) lace to the right side of one body section, so that the bound edges of the lace meet along the center front line. Stitch. Pin lace to the lower edge of the right side of each body section, placing the

113

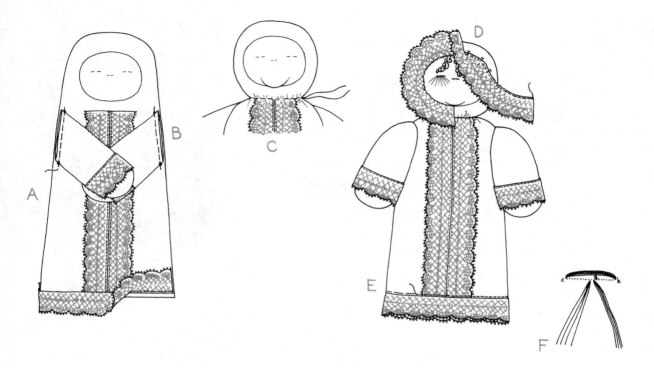

bound edge of the lace ¼"
(6mm) above the lower edge
with the scalloped edge of the
lace toward the top of the
body. Stitch. Press the lace
down and the seam up toward
the doll. Baste the arms to the
front of the doll, matching
small • 's (B).

4 With right sides together,
stitch the body sections together, leaving the bottom
edge open and being careful to
catch in the seam only the basted raw edges of the arms.

5 Turn the doll right side out.
With heavy-duty thread, gather
(see Gathering, p. 33) the neck
by hand along the stitching

line. Stuff the head firmly. Pull
the gathering stitches up
slightly, adding more fiberfill
as necessary to create a chin in
the front. Now, pull up the
gathering stitches as tightly as
possible. Double-knot the
thread ends and trim (C).

6 Cut 3 or 4 strands of yarn,
each 2½" (5.7cm) long. Fold the
strands in half and tack (see
Hand Sewing, p. 34) the folded
edges to the top of the placement line on the head. Gather
a 21" (53.5cm) piece of 1¼"
(32mm) lace by hand, along the
bound edge. Pin the lace to the
face, placing the bound edge
over the placement line and
covering the tacked edges of
the yarn, adjusting the gathers

evenly. Sew the lace in place
by hand (D).

7 Stuff the body with fiberfill.
Baste the bottom edges together just above the lace.
Stitch (E). Tie ⅞ yd (0.80m) of
⅜" (10mm) ribbon into a bow
around the neck.

8 Using 4 strands of brown
embroidery floss, insert the
needle into the center of the
eye stitching line, leaving ¾"
(20mm) of floss hanging (a),
and bring the needle out on the
right end of the stitching line
(b). Then insert the needle on
the left end of the stitching line
(c), and bring it out at the cen-

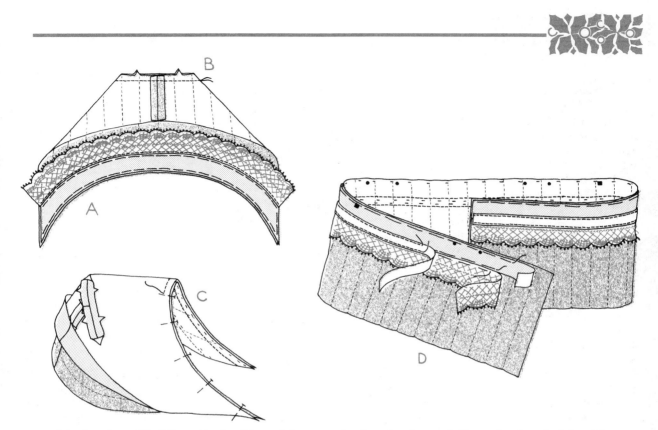

ter (a), leaving ¾″ (20mm) of floss hanging (F). Separate the strands and trim to an arc shape. Use white glue to anchor the strands in place.

9 Using 3 strands of pink embroidery floss, make 3 or 4 small straight stitches on the nose stitching line.

10 Use powder blush to create doll's cheeks.

Carrier

1 Baste the wrong side of the hood band to the right side of the quilted hood. Pin 1¼″ (32mm) lace to the hood, placing the bound edge of the lace along the upper edge of the band (A).

2 Stitch the center back seam of the quilted hood, right sides together. Open the hood out and pin and stitch the remaining notched edges together (B).

3 For the contrast hood, stitch the center back and notched seams as in step 2. Pin the contrast hood to the quilted hood, right sides together. Stitch the front curved edge, leaving the lower edge open (C).

4 Turn the hood right side out. Baste the lower raw edges together. Pin a strip of ⅜″ (10mm) ribbon over the edge of the lace on the hood. Stitch close to both long edges of the ribbon.

5 Baste the wrong side of the carrier side band to the right side of the prequilted carrier side piece, matching symbols. Pin the bound edge of a strip of 1¼″ (32mm) flat lace along the lower edge of the side band. Baste. Center a strip of ribbon over the band and lace, as for the hood, and stitch close to both long edges of the ribbon (D).

6 Stitch the short ends of the side, right sides together.

7 Turn in ¼" (6mm) on the long edges of each strap. Press. Fold each strap in half lengthwise, wrong sides together. Baste. Stitch close to both long edges of each strap.

8 Pin the straps to the side, centering the ends between the symbols and matching raw edges. Baste. Pin the quilted carrier bottom to the side, right sides together, matching large ● 's to the center seam and center. Stitch (E).

9 Turn the carrier right side out. Pin the raw edge of the hood to the side, quilted fabric sides together, and matching center seams and points of the hood to ■ 's. Stitch (F).

10 Trim ¼" (6mm) from the lower edge of the side lining. Stitch the center seam, right sides together, along the short sides.

11 Pin the lining bottom to the side, right sides together, as for the carrier (step 8), matching the large ● 's to the seam and center. Stitch.

12 Turn the carrier wrong side out. Pin the lining to the carrier, right sides together,

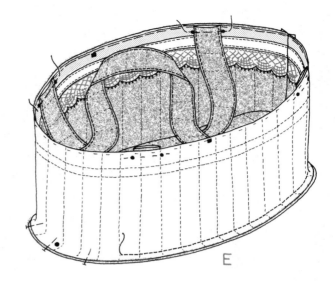

E

matching symbols and seams, having the hood and straps inside between the carrier and the lining. Stitch, leaving an opening between the straps at the hood end, and making sure only the ends of the straps are caught in the seam (G).

13 Turn the carrier right side out. Turn in the raw edges ¼" (6mm) and slipstitch (see Hand Sewing, p. 34) the opening. Stitch through all thicknesses all around the side, just above the ribbon.

Coverlet

1 With right sides together, sew the quilted coverlet to the lining, leaving one entire side open. Trim the corners and turn right side out. Press.

2 Pin the bound edge of the ⅜" (10mm) lace along the seamed edges of the coverlet, beginning and ending the lace ³⁄₁₆" (5mm) from the raw edges.

3 Pin ribbon over the bound edge of the lace, folding in the fullness at the corners (A). Stitch close to both long edges of the ribbon.

4 Turn the raw edges down ⅝" (15mm) to the lining side. Press. Pin the bound edge of a strip of ⅜" (10mm) lace along the raw edges, turning under ½" (13mm) at each end. Baste. Center ribbon over the bound edge of the lace, turning ends under ½" (13mm). Stitch close to both long edges of the ribbon through all thicknesses (B).

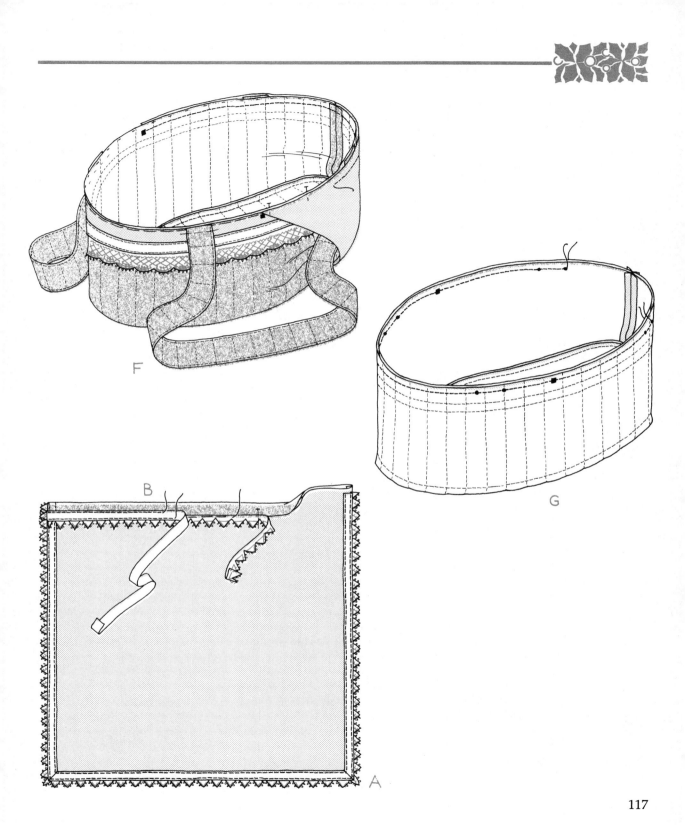

F

G

B

A

117

Desk Accessories:

BRIEFCASE, PENCIL CASE, AND PICTURE FRAME

Make the briefcase, pencil case, or picture frame alone or make them all as a set, for home or office. They are truly handsome gifts when made in synthetic suede or leather. The pencil case can be enlarged an inch in height and width to become an eyeglass case; and the picture frame can be decorated with trim. Add a shoulder strap to the sides of the briefcase to make the carrying easier.

Finished sizes: briefcase—11¼″ × 15¼″ (25cm × 39cm); pencil case—2½″ × 6″ (6cm × 15cm); frame—8″ × 10″ (20cm × 25cm).

MATERIALS NEEDED

Briefcase
⅝ yd (0.60m) of 35″ or 45″ (90cm or 115cm) fabric and lining
16½″ × 32″ (42cm × 81cm) polyester batting remnant
6″ × 9½″ (15cm × 24cm) Aida cloth no. 14 remnant
6″ × 9″ (15cm × 23cm) fusible web remnant
10¾″ × 15¼″ (27.3cm × 39cm) mat board
¾ yd (0.70m) of ¼″ (6mm) velvet ribbon
¾ yd (0.70m) of ⅜″ (10mm) upholstery cord
4 skeins of contrast embroidery floss
one ¾″ (20mm) self-gripping fastener

Picture frame
10″ × 12″ (25cm × 30cm) remnant for front
9″ × 11″ (23cm × 28cm) remnant for back
18″ × 22″ (46cm × 56cm) polyester batting remnant
11″ × 18″ (28cm × 46cm) mat board
⅛ yd (0.20m) of ⅜″ (10mm) ribbon

Pencil holder
7″ × 7″ (18cm × 18cm) fabric remnant
7″ × 7″ (18cm × 18cm) lining remnant
7″ × 7″ (18cm × 18cm) polyester batting remnant

¼ yd (0.30m) of ¼″ (6mm) decorative trim
2 skeins of contrast embroidery floss

Pattern pieces are found on p. 176.

CUTTING INFORMATION

Briefcase
Fabric: 1 briefcase
Lining: 1 briefcase
Polyester batting: 1 briefcase
Fusible web: 1 rectangle 4″ × 7½″ (10cm × 19cm)

Picture frame
Fabric remnant: 1 frame
Lining remnant: 1 Guide B
Polyester batting: 2 Guide A
Mat board: 1 Guide A; 1 Guide B; 1 Stand

Pencil holder
Fabric remnant: 2 pencil holders
Lining remnant: 2 pencil holders
Polyester batting: 2 pencil holders

HOW-TO

All seam allowances are ¼″ (6mm).

Briefcase

1 On the Aida cloth, turn under the raw edges ½″ (13mm) all around and baste close to the edges, or machine zigzag the raw edges. Center your letters and borders (see Monograms, p. 183) on the cloth according to the cloth's finished size, 4″ × 7½″ (10cm × 19cm). Use 3 strands of floss in a cross stitch for letters and 6 separated strands in a gobelin stitch for the border (see Embroidery, p. 25).

2 Trim the Aida cloth to 4″ × 7½″ (10cm × 19cm). Place the embroidered Aida cloth over the fusible web, centering both on the right side of the briefcase ¾″ (20mm) above the upper foldline and 4⅜″ (11cm) in from each side. Fuse the monogram in place lightly, following manufacturer's directions and without pressing the needlework flat. Stitch close to the outer edges of the Aida cloth. Position the loop side of the self-gripping fastener to the right side of the briefcase 2¾″ (7cm) below the middle foldline and 8⅛″ (21cm) in from each side. Stitch.

3 Baste the batting to the wrong side of the briefcase, ⅛″ (3mm) from the outer edges. Fold the briefcase, right sides together, along the middle foldline. Stitch the sides to the large ● 's (A). Turn the briefcase right side out.

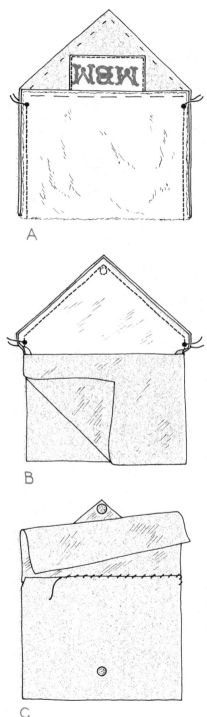

A

B

C

4 Cut off 1¾″ (4.5cm) from the lower straight edge of the lining. Sew the hook side of the self-gripping fastener to the right side of the lining ⅝″ (15mm) below the point. Fold the lining, right sides together, along the middle foldline. Stitch the sides.

5 Turn the lining right side out. Pin the lining flap to the briefcase flap, right sides together. Stitch between the large ● 's (B).

6 Turn the flap and lining right side out. Insert the mat board into the front of the briefcase, through the lining opening. Slipstitch (see Hand Sewing, p. 34) the lining in place to the front of the briefcase (C).

7 Turn the lining into the briefcase so that the wrong side of the lining is next to the batting side of the briefcase, folding the upper straight edge of the front to the inside at the foldline.

8 Place velvet ribbon around the outer edge of the monogrammed Aida cloth, folding the ribbon corners into miters (see Corners for Trims, p. 24), and, gluing the ribbon in place as you go, trim off excess ribbon. Glue or hand sew upholstery cord to the edge of the front flap. Flatten the raw ends slightly and glue or sew them to the inside flap. If the ends are glued, weight them down with heavy objects until they dry.

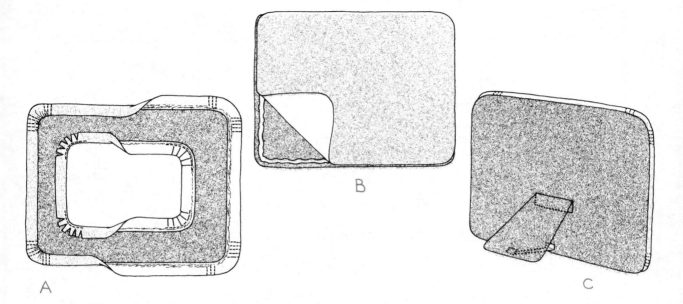

A

B

C

Picture Frame

1 On the right side of the frame, make 5 rows of top-stitching across the 2 long sides, stitching the first row 1" (25mm) in from the raw edges and the next 4 rows ¼" (6mm) apart, stitching toward the center. Make 3 rows of topstitching across the 2 short sides, stitching the first row 1¼" (3.2cm) in from the raw edges and the next 2 rows ¼" (6mm) apart, stitching toward the center.

2 Reinforce the inner corners of the frame with a line of stitching along the foldline, using small machine stitches.

Clip the corners to the stitching.

3 Center both layers of batting on the wrong side of the frame. Place the mat board cut from Guide A on top of the batting. Fold the outer raw edges of the frame over the mat board, easing in the fabric at the outer corners. Glue in place and let glue dry thoroughly. Fold the inner corners of the frame over the mat board, stretching taut and making sure the clips at the corners will not show on the right side. Glue in place, one side at a time. Secure with large paper clips until dry (A).

4 Glue the edges of the wrong side of the back fabric to the mat board cut from Guide B (B).

5 Position the wrong side of the frame to the mat board cut from Guide B, and glue around the outer edges, leaving one side or the top open for inserting the picture.

6 Score the foldline of the stand with a mat knife, cutting only the surface of the mat board. Glue the small area above the foldline on the stand to the back of the frame at the placement lines (C).

7 Turn the stand down after the glue is dry. Cut 1 piece of ribbon 3½" (9cm). Turn in the ends of the ribbon ½" (13mm). Center and glue the ends over the large ● 's on the back of the frame and on the stand.

Pencil Holder

1 On the right side of one pencil holder, machine stitch 12 rows, each ⅜″ (10mm) apart, using 8 stitches per inch (per 25mm).

2 Starting at the bottom edge of the top row of stitching and using 6 strands of embroidery floss, do a threaded running stitch (see Embroidery, p. 25), as shown, through every other machine stitch. Repeat on alternate rows of machine stitching.

3 Using 6 strands of a second color, thread the running stitch between the top, middle, and bottom pairs of stitching rows (A).

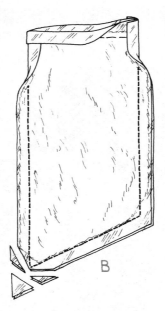

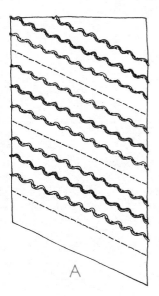

4 Stitch the pencil holder sections, right sides together, along the sides and diagonal bottom, leaving the top straight edge open. Trim across corners and turn right side out. Press.

5 Trim ¼″ (6mm) from upper edge of each batting section. Pin and baste the batting to the wrong side of each lining section, placing the upper edge of the batting ¼″ (6mm) below the upper edge of the lining. Stitch the lining sections, right sides together, along the sides and bottom, leaving the top straight edge open. Trim across corners.

6 Turn in ¼″ (6mm) on the top edge of the lining to the wrong side. Press (B).

7 Insert the lining into the pencil holder so that the raw edge of the case is even with the pressed edge of the lining. Stitch lining and case together ⅛″ (3mm) from the edge.

8 Starting and ending at the back of the pencil holder, glue upholstery trim to the upper outer edge, with the trim extending slightly beyond the top edge of the fabric.

Bed Caddy

A practical, delightful gift, this bed caddy can be made in whatever fabric suits the room it will be used in—from satin to broadcloth, gingham to chintz. Why not make the bed caddy to match your bedspread and drapes, or decorate it with bands from your bedspread and drapery fabric? This is a thoughtful gift to whip up and fill with reading matter if a loved one is confined to bed with an illness, or to fill with small toys and puzzles for a child. For a more masculine touch, substitute braid for the lace beading.

Finished size: 17½" long × 12½" wide (44cm × 32cm).

MATERIALS NEEDED

1½ yd (1.40m) of 45" (115cm) fabric *or* 1¾ yd (1.60cm) of 35" (90cm) fabric

15" × 19½" (38cm × 50cm) remnant of polyester batting

½ yd (0.50m) of matching or contrast fabric for self bias *or* 1¾ yds (1.60m) of wide bias tape for binding (optional)

1¼ yds (1.15m) of 1" (25mm) lace or eyelet beading with ribbon 8" × 13" (21cm × 33cm) cardboard

Pattern pieces are found on pp. 177-178.

CUTTING INFORMATION

Fabric: two 15" × 19½" (38cm × 49.5cm) rectangles; 1 pocket A; 2 pocket B; 2 pocket C; 2 pocket D

Polyester batting remnant: one 15" × 19½" (38cm × 49.5cm) rectangle

Cardboard: 1 pocket A

HOW-TO

All seam allowances are ⅝" (15mm).

1 Sandwich the batting between the wrong sides of the 2 large rectangular pieces. Baste. Machine quilt in parallel rows, ⅞" (22mm) apart (see Quilting, p. 40). Cut out 1 bed caddy from this quilted piece.

2 Turn in the straight edge of pocket A ⅝" (15mm), turning under ¼" (6mm) on the raw edge. Stitch. Pin the wrong side of this pocket to the sides and lower edge of the bed caddy. Baste as shown (A).

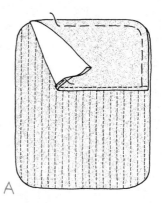

A

3 With wrong sides together, pin pocket B sections together. Baste around all edges. Trim 1 straight upper seam allowance to 3⁄16" (5mm), and the remaining one to ⅜" (10mm). Fold the ⅜" (10mm) seam allowance over the 3⁄16" (5mm) seam allowance, along the seamline, enclosing the raw edges. Baste and press (B).

122

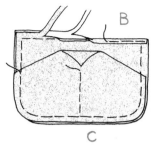

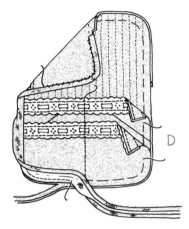

4 With right sides together, stitch the pocket C sections along the upper pointed edges. Trim the seam and turn the pocket right side out. Baste the sides and lower curved edges together.

5 Pin pocket C to the outside of pocket B, matching raw edges. Baste (C).

6 Pin the beading over the upper edge of pocket B, covering the basted seam allowances and the point of pocket C, with raw edges even at the sides. Stitch close to both long edges of the beading.

7 Prepare pocket D the same way as pocket B, step 3. Stitch beading to the upper edge as in step 6.

8 Pin pocket D to the outside of pocket C, matching lower raw edges. Baste. Stitch through the center through all thicknesses.

9 Pin the pockets to the remaining side of the bed caddy (pocket A is on the other side). Baste (D).

10 If you are using self bias, make bias strips (see Bias Binding, p. 19) 1⅜″ (3.5cm) wide. Turn in ¼″ (6mm) on both long edges and press. Encase the other raw edges of the caddy with bias (see Bias Binding, p. 19).

11 Trim ¾″ (20mm) from the sides and lower edges of the cardboard. Insert it into pocket A.

12 Remove the ribbon from the leftover beading. Tie it into a bow and tack it to the center of the beading on pocket B (see photo).

Padded Hanger and Hanger Cover

When you take the time and care to make a beautiful fashion garment, doesn't it deserve to hang on a padded hanger, protected from harm with a hanger cover? These hangers are pretty to look at and a delight to use. Make a few for yourself when you make them as gifts for family and friends. Decorate them with artificial flowers or ribbon roses for an extra touch of elegance. Cover your wooden hangers in piqué, satin, moiré, broadcloth, or chintz—or turn the hanger cover into the perfect garment dust cover by making it in soft plastic.

Finished sizes: padded hanger—approximately ¾″ × 16″ (20mm × 40cm); hanger cover— 8¾″ high × 20″ long × 2″ deep (22cm × 51cm × 5cm).

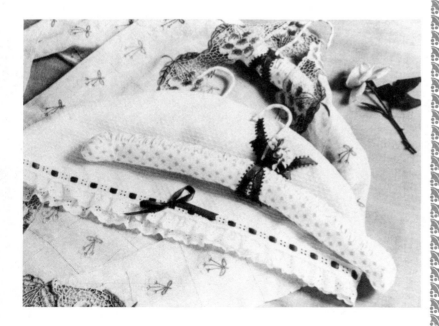

MATERIALS NEEDED

Padded hanger

¼ yd (0.30m) of 45″ (115cm) fabric

¾ yd (0.70cm) of ½″ (13mm) ribbon

4 oz (120 grams) of polyester fiberfill

1 wooden dress hanger, approximately ¾″ × 16″ (20mm × 40cm)

1 small artificial flower or ribbon rose [⅛ yd. (0.15m) of 1½″ (38mm) ribbon]

Hanger cover

½ yd (0.50m) of 45″ (115cm) fabric

1⅜ yds (1.30m) of 2″ (50mm) single-edged ruffle beading with ribbon

¼ yd (0.30m) of ¼″ (6mm) ribbon to match beading

Pattern pieces are found on p. 179.

CUTTING INFORMATION

Padded hanger

Fabric: 2 hanger tops; 2 hanger bottoms; 1½″ (38mm) wide bias strip the length of the hanger hook plus ½″ (13mm)

Hanger cover

Fabric: 2 hanger covers; 1 hanger cover gusset

HOW-TO

All seam allowances are ⅝" (15mm).

Padded Hanger

1 Turn in ⅝" (15mm) on the short straight end of each hanger top and hanger bottom. Baste in place.

2 Make two rows of gathering stitches (see Gathering, p. 33) in the seam allowance along the long sides of each hanger top section from the basted end to within 1¼" (3.2cm) of the rounded end (A).

3 With right sides together, pin 1 hanger top to 1 hanger bottom, pulling up and adjusting the gathers to fit. Stitch (B),

leaving the straight short end open. Trim seams and turn right side out.

4 Fold the bias strip, right sides together, in half lengthwise. Stitch ½" (13mm) seam on one short end and along the long raw edges. Trim, turn right side out and press. Slip the bias tube over the hook section of the hanger.

5 Stuff a small amount of fiberfill into the end of each hanger section, using the eraser end of a pencil. Slip the hanger sections over each arm of the hanger, with the gathered side on top. Finish stuffing each section with fiberfill (C).

6 Slipstitch (see Hand Sewing, p. 34) the basted edge of the sections together and then slipstitch the bias cover on the hanger hook to the hanger cover.

7 Cut the ends of the ribbon diagonally. Wrap it around the center of the hanger twice and tie the ends into a bow. Make a medium ribbon rose (see Gift Wrapping, p. 129) or use a purchased flower; tack (see Hand Sewing, p. 34) to the top of the hanger (see photo)

125

Hanger Cover

1 Cut a ½″ × 1½″ (13mm × 3.8cm) section of fabric. Baste it in place on the wrong side of the gusset, 15⅝″ (39.5cm) from one end for reinforcement. On the right side of the gusset, make a 1″ (25mm) buttonhole.

2 Pin and stitch the hanger cover sections to each long side of the gusset, right sides together. Stitch again, ¼″ (6mm) away from the first stitching in the seam allowance; trim close to the stitching. Turn right side out (A).

3 Turn the lower edge of the cover to the outside ⅝″ (15mm); baste close to the fold. Trim the basted seam allowance to ¼″ (6mm).

4 Starting at the center of one long side, pin the beading over the turned-up edge. Turn under the end of the beading ½″ (13mm) and lap the remaining raw end. Stitch close to both long edges of the beading, stitching down across the lapped end (B).

5 Trim the ends of the ¼″ (6mm) ribbon diagonally. Tie it (B) into a bow and tack it to the hanger cover at the overlapped beading.

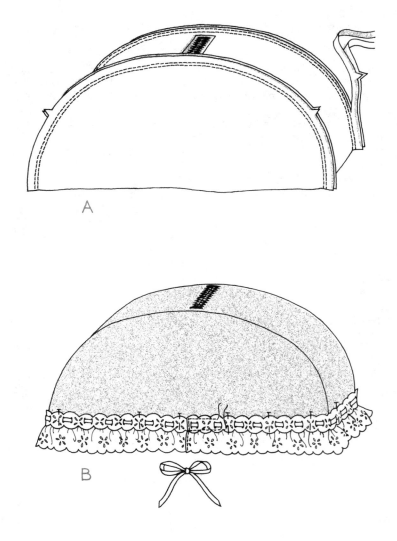

A

B

Casserole and Oven Mitts

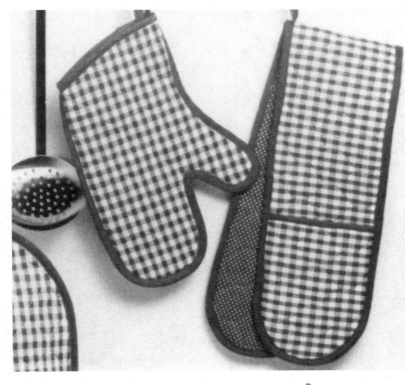

JONES NEW YORK
AT HOME

A cinch to make and always a welcome gift to receive—what cook wouldn't appreciate a matching set of oven and casserole mitts? You can use double-faced prequilted fabric or quilt your own. Make a matching set to go with the Holiday Appliquéd Apron for your favorite holiday cook, or make a number of sets to sell during the busy charity bazaar season. Useful all year long, these kitchen helpers move outdoors as a nice hostess gift to say thanks for summer weekend visits.

Finished sizes: casserole mitt—36″ (91.5cm) long; oven mitt—14″ (35.5cm) long.

MATERIALS NEEDED

Casserole and oven mitts

⅝ yd (0.60m) of 45″ (115cm) double-faced prequilted fabric

4⅛ yds (3.80m) of extra wide bias tape *or* ⅞″ (22mm) wide bias tape

Pattern pieces are found on p. 180.

CUTTING INFORMATION

Fabric: 1 casserole mitt; 2 casserole mitt pockets; 2 oven mitts

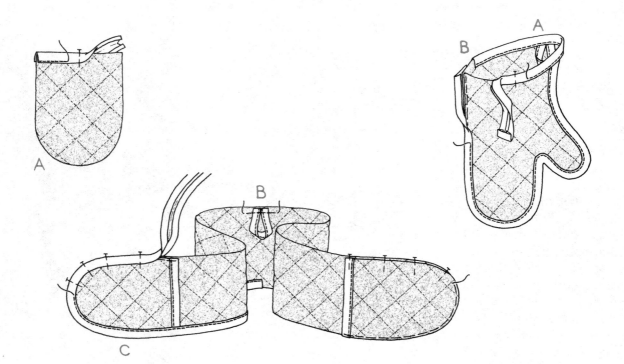

HOW-TO

Casserole Mitt

1 Cut two 6" (15cm) strips of bias tape.

2 Encase the top straight edge of the pocket sections with the tape (A). (See Bias Binding, p. 19.)

3 Cut a 4" (10cm) strip of bias tape and stitch the long folded edges together. Place the raw ends together to form a loop. Center the loop on the wrong side of the mitt and baste it in place, having the raw edges of the loop match the raw edges of the mitt (B).

4 Pin the wrong side of the pockets to the right side of the mitt, 1 at each end. Baste ¼" (6mm) from the raw edges.

5 Encase the raw edges with bias tape (C). Pin and stitch.

Oven Mitt

1 Make a loop as for the casserole mitt, step 3. Baste the loop near the upper corner of the wrong side of one oven mitt section (A).

2 Pin the oven mitt sections, wrong sides together, and baste ¼" (6mm) from the edges, leaving the end open.

3 Encase the basted edges with bias tape. Pin and stitch. Encase the remaining open end edges with bias tape, beginning at the side opposite the loop (B). Pin and stitch.

Gift Wrapping

After you've worked hard to make a gift, this special item deserves extra attention when it comes to wrapping. Crafters with special skills in handwork will find these ideas appropriate and adaptable for gifts for occasions all year long.

BOXING YOUR GIFT

If you don't have a gift box on hand, many department stores and five-and-dimes offer them for sale. For large items check your local supermarket, liquor store, or drugstore. The most important criterion is that the box be at least as large as the gift you need to wrap.

WRAPPING PAPER

There are endless varieties of commercial gift wrapping paper available. But for more creative and unusual ways to wrap gifts consider these options:

Newspaper

Yes, newspaper. The sheets are large and readily available. To make it special, match the section of the newspaper to the person or gift. For example, if the gift is a tie for a businessman, wrap it in the stock market reports. A child's toy, wrap with the comics. If your gift is for a stylish woman, use a big fashion ad.

Fabrics

Here's a useful way to get rid of fabric scraps. Cut squares or rectangles of fabric for wrapping, using pinking shears.

Fabric bags, too, are a nice way to wrap a gift in a gift. Cut a rectangle of fabric, fold it in half, wrong sides together, and stitch across the bottom and up the cut side to a point 1¼" (3.2cm) down from the top open edge. Leaving a ½" (13mm) opening, continue stitching the last ¾" (20mm) to the top edge. Finish the raw edge by turning under ⅛" (3mm) and stitching, then turn the top edge ⅝" (15mm) to the inside, and stitch the edge ½" (13mm) from the fold, forming a casing. Using a bodkin, insert ribbon through the seam opening for a drawstring.

Making a simple bow

Often a pretty ribbon or a very wide one, tied into a simple bow, makes the most smashing decoration of all. Here's how to do it:

Trim the ends of ribbon diagonally. Or notch the ends of wide ribbon by folding the end in half lengthwise, and making a diagonal cut from the outside edges toward the folded side.

Aluminum foil

Why not? It is an especially good gift wrapping for holiday gifts for your favorite gourmet cook.

No paper at all

There are some gifts that are too big or too oddly shaped to wrap. Forget about trying. Cut out felt or paper Christmas shapes—bells, trees, stars, etc.—and glue or tape them on the box to decorate it and to cover any revealing labels or printing. Or if the box has no printing, draw designs or holiday scenes on it.

TIE IT UP

There's a lot of craft ribbon you can buy by the reel. These pretty ribbons are mostly formed material, not woven, and can be used only for wrapping gifts, not for sewing. But if you have special gift wrap, why not have special ties and trims? Gold or silver cording or middy braid and satin macramé cord make very elegant gift ties. One cord tied one time around a beautifully wrapped box adds a crowning touch to a special gift.

Several strands of leftover yarn, the same or different colors, make an interesting gift tie-up.

There are really no rules as to what you can use to tie up a package. For example, if the gift is a garment, buckle a matching belt around the package, or tie up a child's gift with a jump rope.

SPECIAL TRIMS

Satin ribbon roses and satin or velvet ribbon leaves look magnificent on top of a gift package when made from good-quality woven ribbon (G).

G

Ribbon roses

For small roses, use 4" (10cm) lengths of 1" (25mm) wide ribbon; for medium roses, use 5" (13cm) lengths of 1½" (38mm) wide ribbon; for large roses, use 9" (23cm) lengths of 3½" (90mm) wide ribbon.

For each rose, fold the right raw edge down to meet the long edge of the ribbon at a 45° angle. Fold the left raw edge down to form a point ¼" (6mm) away from the lower edge (H). Make a row of hand gathering stitches (see Gathering, p. 33) along the lower edge, securing the folded ends (I). Gather 1" (25mm) wide ribbon to a length of 1½" (3.8cm); 1½" (38mm) wide ribbon to a length of 2" (5cm); and 3½" (90mm) wide ribbon to a length of 3" (7.5cm). Beginning with the right end of the gathered ribbon, roll it along the gathered edge, tacking (see Hand Sewing, p. 34) the roll at the gathered edge. Turn the left end under, even with the lower edge, fastening it with several whipstitches (see Hand Sewing, p. 34) over the edge (J).

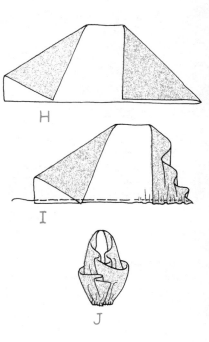

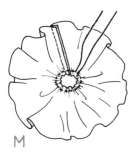

Ribbon leaves

For small leaves, cut 1" (25mm) wide ribbon into 1¼" (3.2cm) strips; for large leaves, cut 1½" (38mm) wide ribbon into 1½" strips. With right sides together, fold the strip in half lengthwise. Whipstitch the short raw edges together at one end. Turn the ribbon right side out, forming a point (K).

Bring the lower raw edges together, forming a pleat. Tack securely (L).

Tie a ribbon around your gift package and make a simple bow. On top of the bow, tack (see Hand Sewing, p. 34) on the roses and leaves.

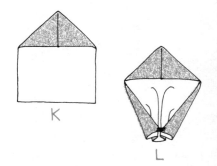

Other ribbon flowers

Another pretty ribbon flower can be made from any kind of woven ribbon. For each flower, cut a 5" to 7" (12.5cm to 18cm) length of ribbon, 1" (25mm) or wider, cutting the wider ribbon into the longer lengths. Join the raw ends, right sides together, in a ¼" (6mm) seam, forming a continuous loop. Along one edge, make a row of hand gathering stitches. Pull up the gathering stitches, forming a flower. Tie the ends of the threads together and trim (M). Tack the flowers to your gift as described for the roses.

Pom-Poms

Frothy pom-poms tied on a gift are great for a child's special
present. Pom-poms make fine finishing touches on hats, as flower
centers, and as decorations anywhere you choose to put them. Use
up your leftover yarn, making them in one color or a mixture of
colors. The amount of yarn you use determines the fullness of the
pom-pom.

   Cut a 2″ × 5″ (5cm × 12.5cm) piece of cardboard. Loosely wind the
yarn around it until you have the amount of fullness you want. Tie
the loops of yarn tightly together with a separate piece of yarn at
one long edge of the cardboard, slipping the yarn tie between the
loops and the cardboard. Cut the loops apart at the opposite long
side for the
pom-pom.

   Smaller or larger pom-poms can be made using larger or smaller
pieces of cardboard.

Basic Shapes

Basic Shapes

Here they all are, the basic Christmas shapes you can make into ornaments, toys, appliqués, or decorations of any kind. These shapes may be used full size, so just trace them onto tracing paper to create a pattern, seam allowances included. If you want to increase or decrease the size, mark off a grid for the shape and one for enlarging (see Enlarging Patterns, page 29).

You can make these shapes from a variety of materials. If you use felt, cut the details from different-colored pieces and glue or zigzag the smaller pieces in place. Make them from woven fabrics, appliquéing the details; sew on a backing and fill with stuffing. You can also transfer all the detail lines to the right side of your fabric and paint in the details with fabric paint. Or mix and match fabrics and textures.

Use these shapes as appliqués on holiday linens, aprons, wall hangings, and garments—or anything you like. You can also use many of the shapes—the bell, heart, and star, for instance—as appliqués on non-Christmas projects. It's a good way for using up fabric scraps, too!

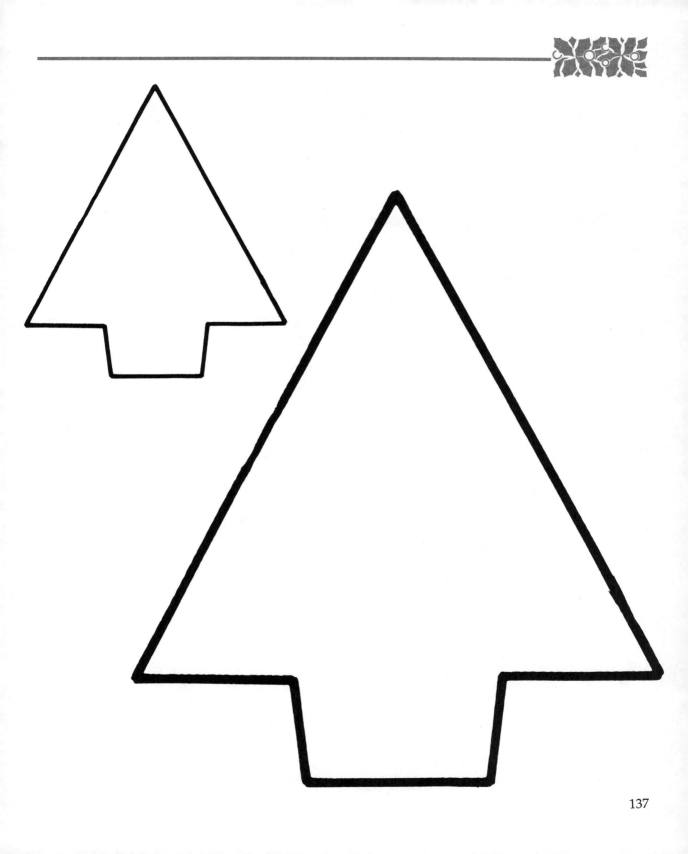

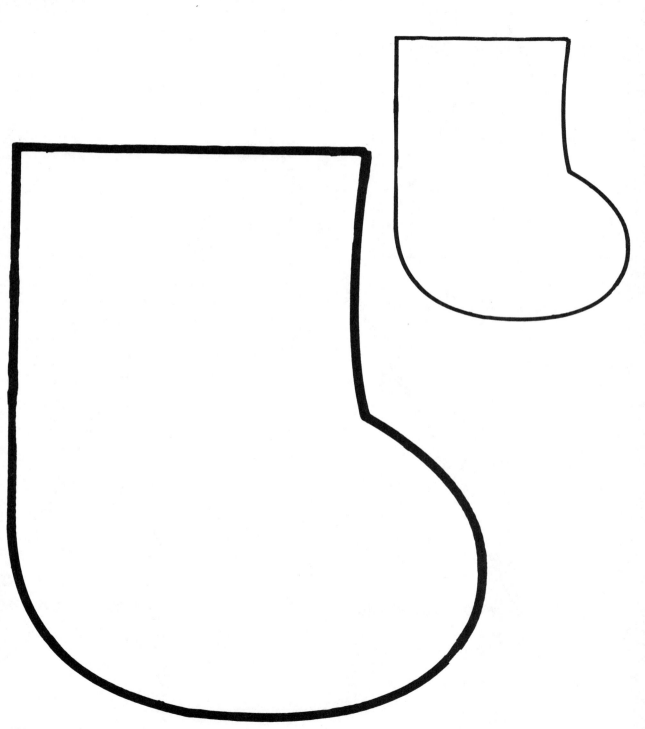

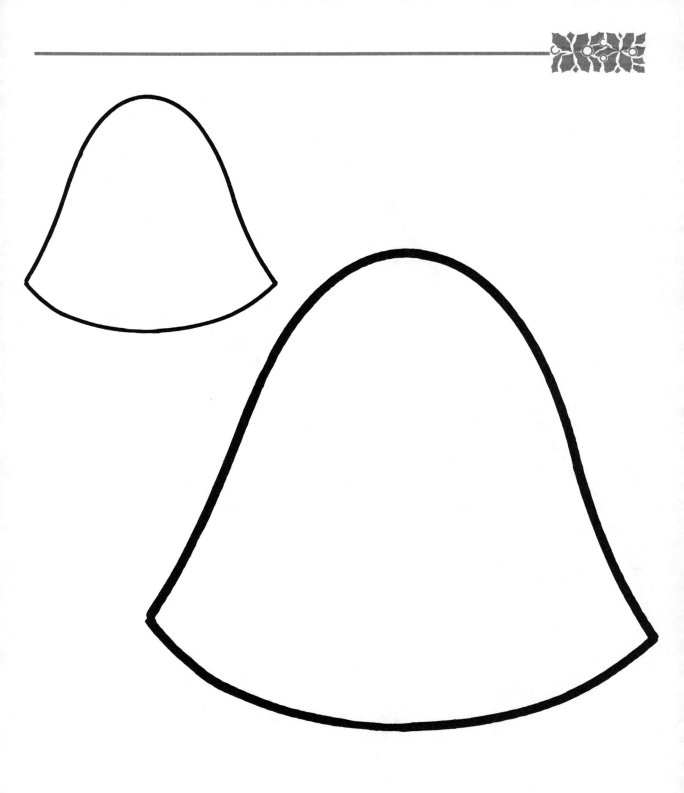

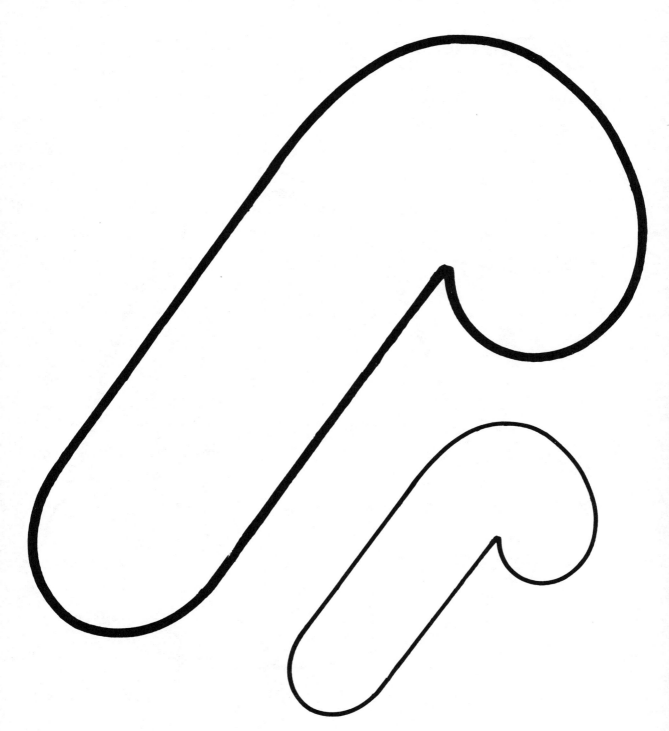

Patterns

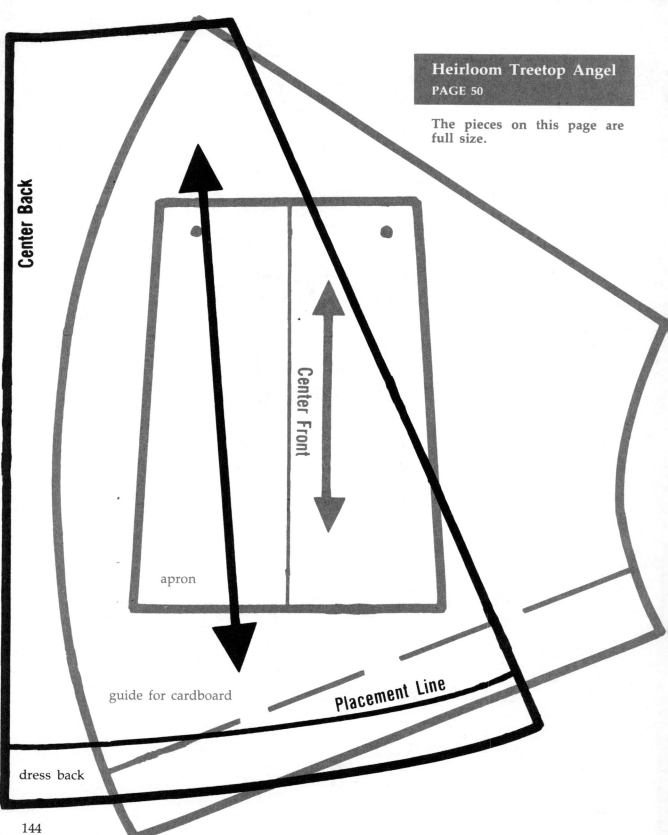

The pieces on this page are full size.

Center Back

Center Front

apron

guide for cardboard

Placement Line

dress back

144

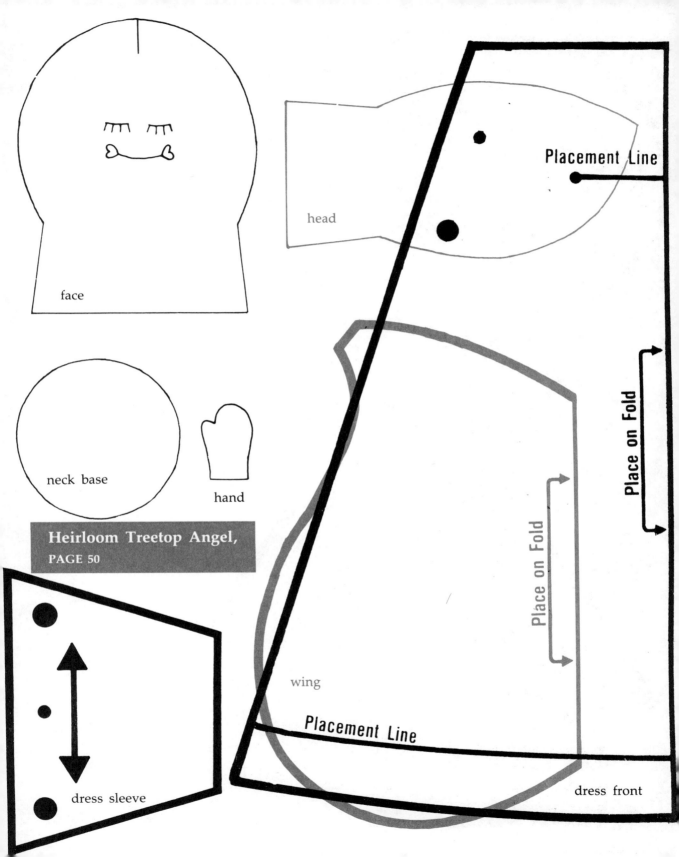

face

head

Placement Line

neck base

hand

Place on Fold

Place on Fold

Heirloom Treetop Angel,
PAGE 50

wing

Placement Line

dress front

dress sleeve

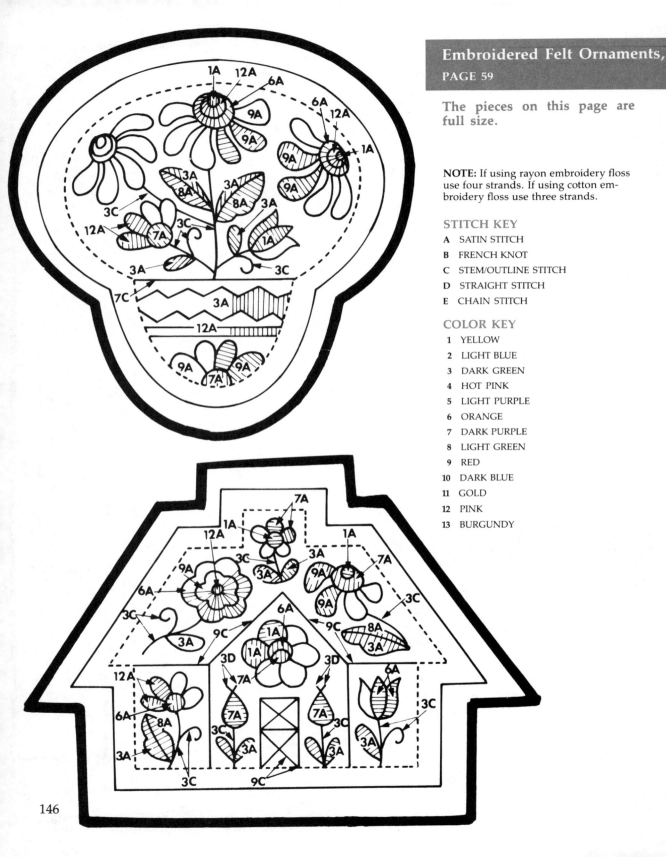

The pieces on this page are full size.

NOTE: If using rayon embroidery floss use four strands. If using cotton embroidery floss use three strands.

STITCH KEY

A SATIN STITCH
B FRENCH KNOT
C STEM/OUTLINE STITCH
D STRAIGHT STITCH
E CHAIN STITCH

COLOR KEY

1 YELLOW
2 LIGHT BLUE
3 DARK GREEN
4 HOT PINK
5 LIGHT PURPLE
6 ORANGE
7 DARK PURPLE
8 LIGHT GREEN
9 RED
10 DARK BLUE
11 GOLD
12 PINK
13 BURGUNDY

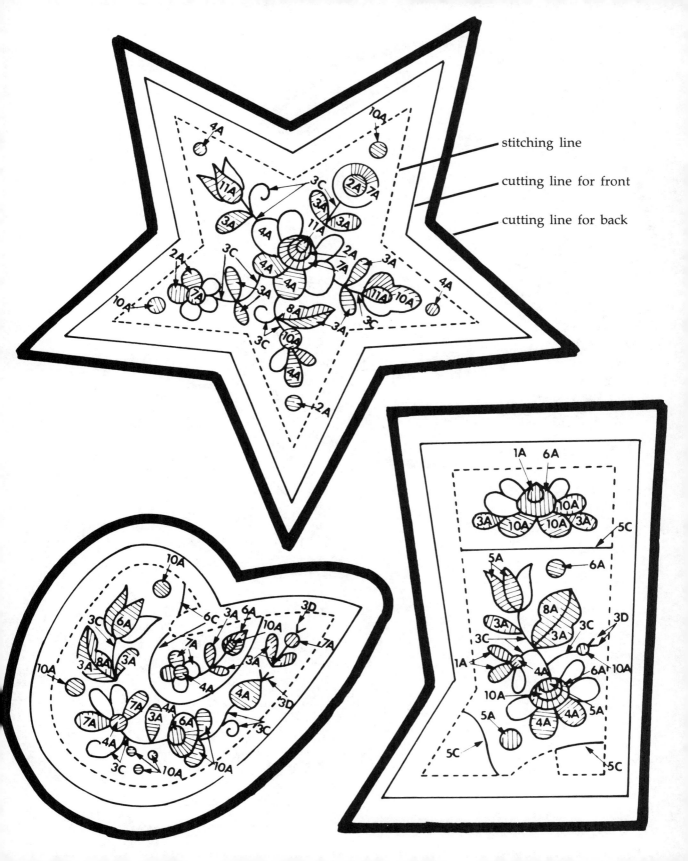

stitching line

cutting line for front

cutting line for back

NOTE: If using rayon embroidery floss use four strands. If using cotton embroidery floss use three strands.

The pieces on this page are full size.

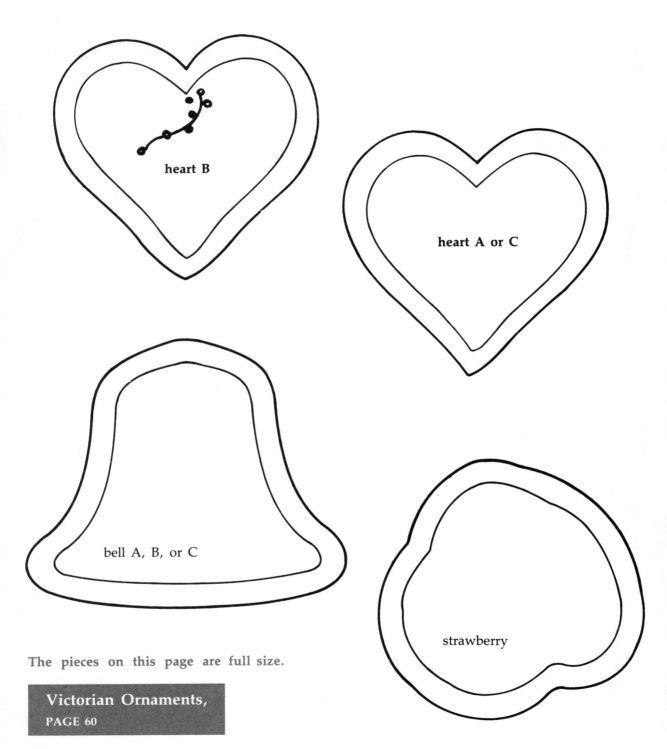

heart B

heart A or C

bell A, B, or C

strawberry

The pieces on this page are full size.

Victorian Ornaments,
PAGE 60

150

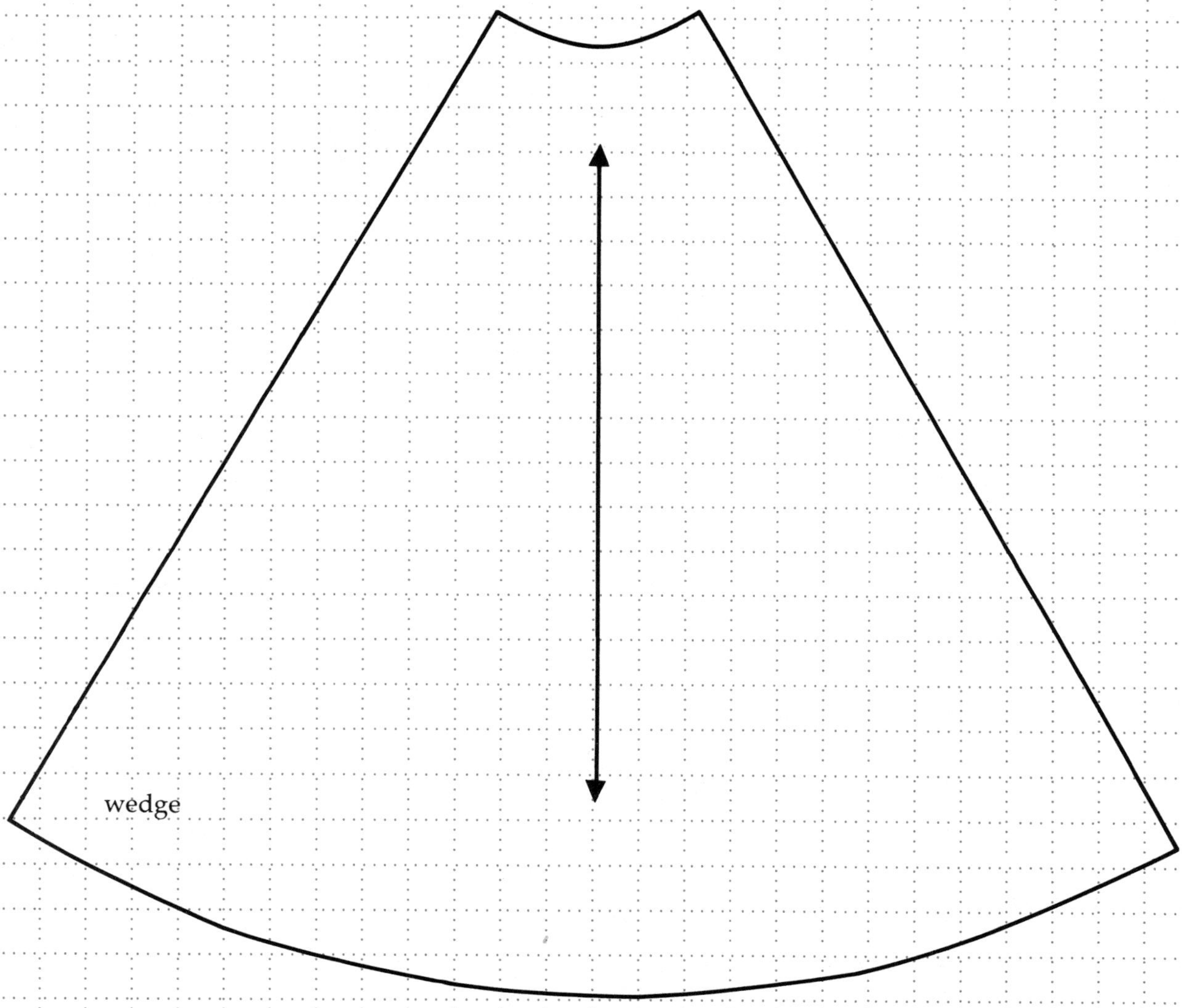

wedge

Tree Skirt,
PAGE 65

1 sq. = 1"

To enlarge pattern pieces to full size
see *Enlarging Patterns,* p. 29.

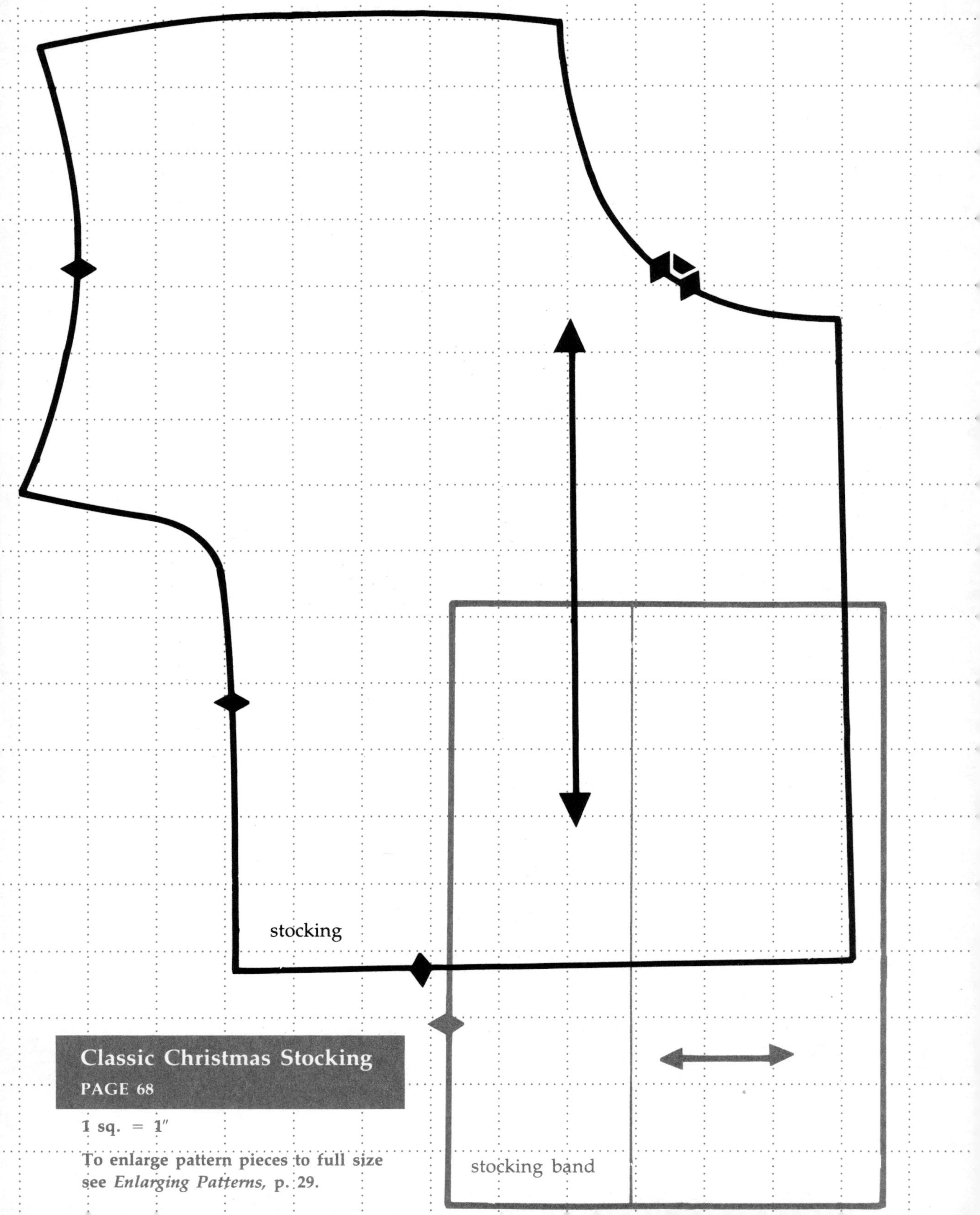

stocking

Classic Christmas Stocking
PAGE 68

1 sq. = 1″

To enlarge pattern pieces to full size see *Enlarging Patterns,* p. 29.

stocking band

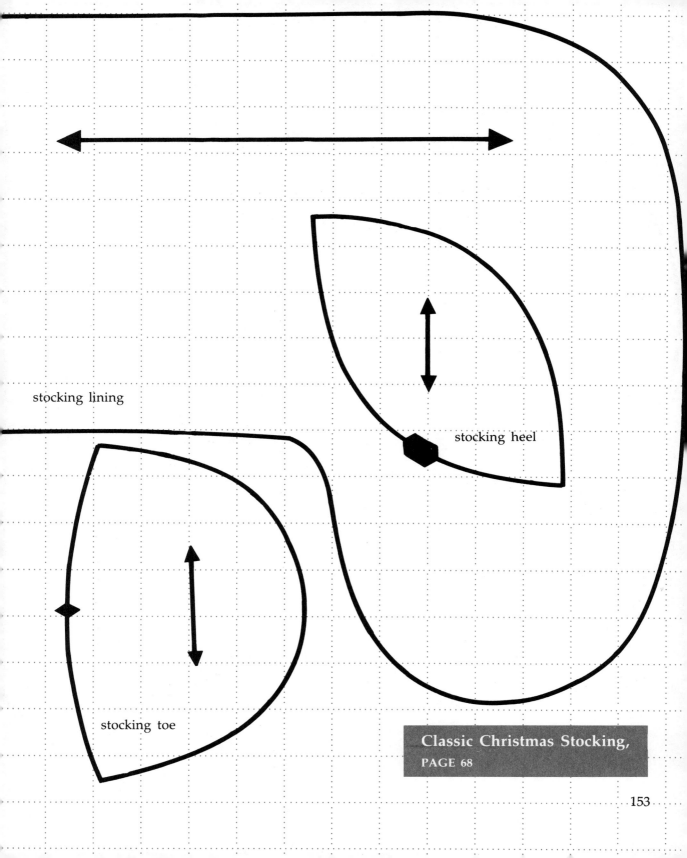

stocking lining

stocking heel

stocking toe

Classic Christmas Stocking,
PAGE 68

153

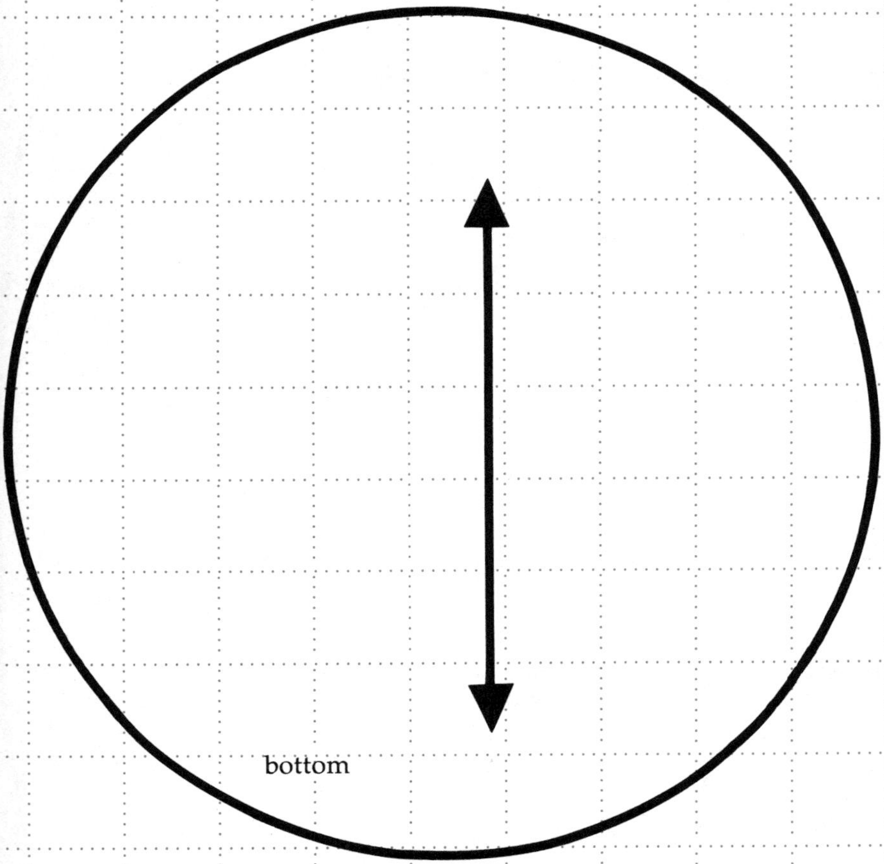

bottom

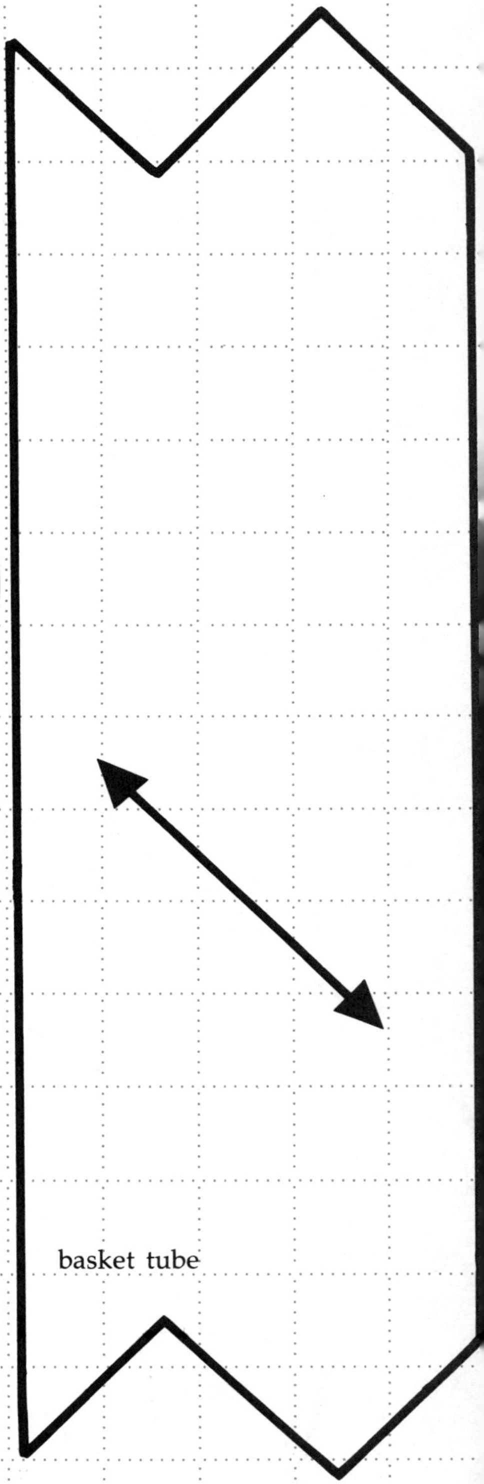

Fabric Basket,
PAGE 77

1 sq. = 1″

To enlarge pattern pieces to full size
see *Enlarging Patterns,* p. 29.

basket tube

154

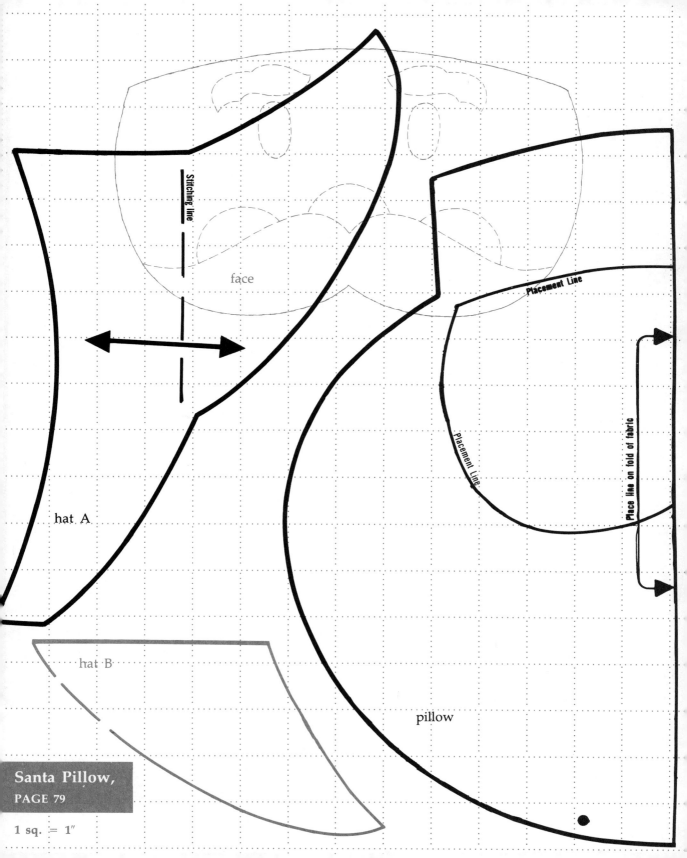

Stitching line

face

Placement Line

Placement Line

Place line on fold of fabric

hat A

hat B

pillow

1 sq. = 1"

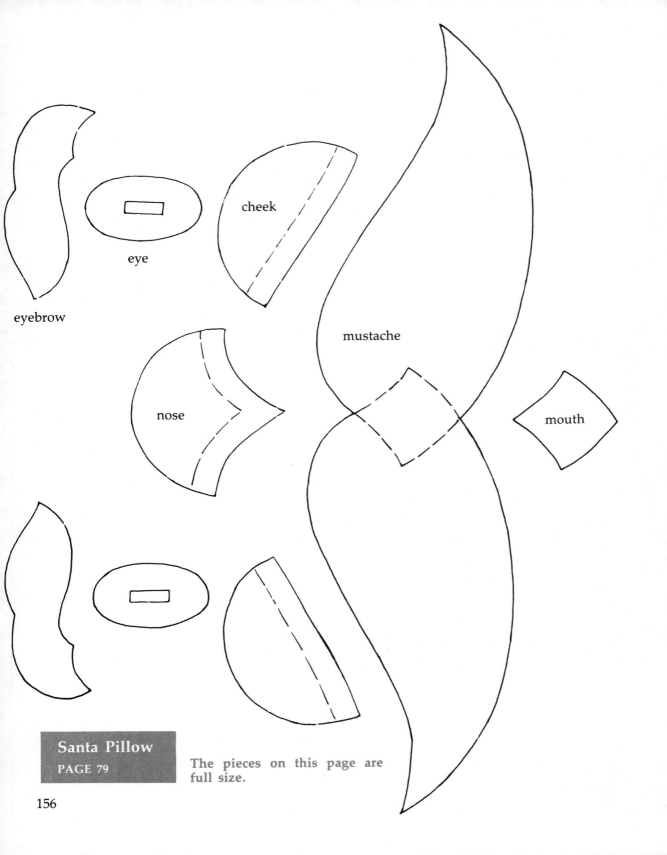

eyebrow

eye

cheek

mustache

nose

mouth

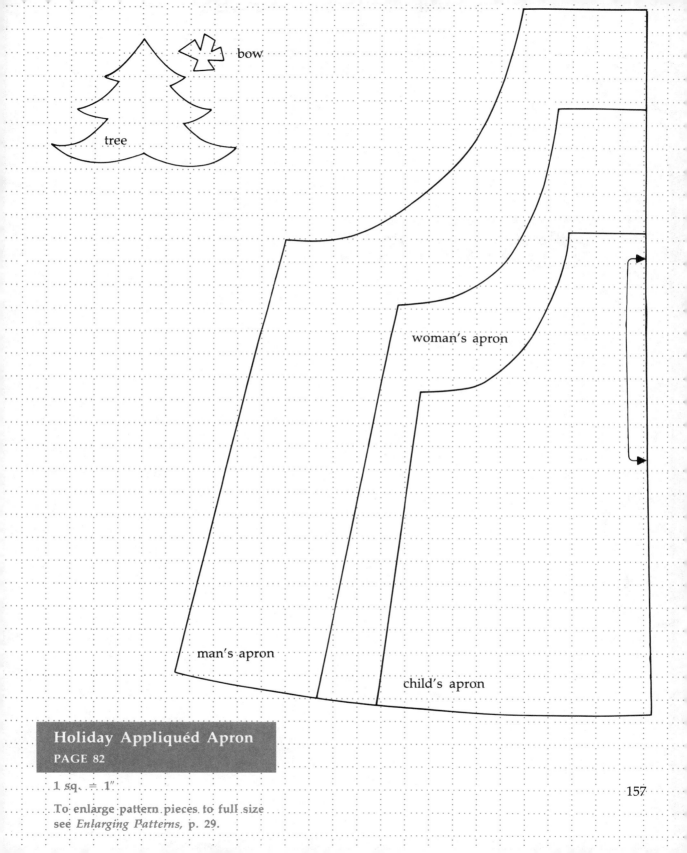

bow

tree

woman's apron

man's apron

child's apron

Holiday Appliquéd Apron
PAGE 82

1 sq. = 1"

To enlarge pattern pieces to full size
see *Enlarging Patterns,* p. 29.

corner guide for table runner

corner guide for placemat

Christmas Table Decorations,
PAGE 84

1 sq. = 1"

To enlarge pattern pieces to full size
see *Enlarging Patterns*, p. 29.

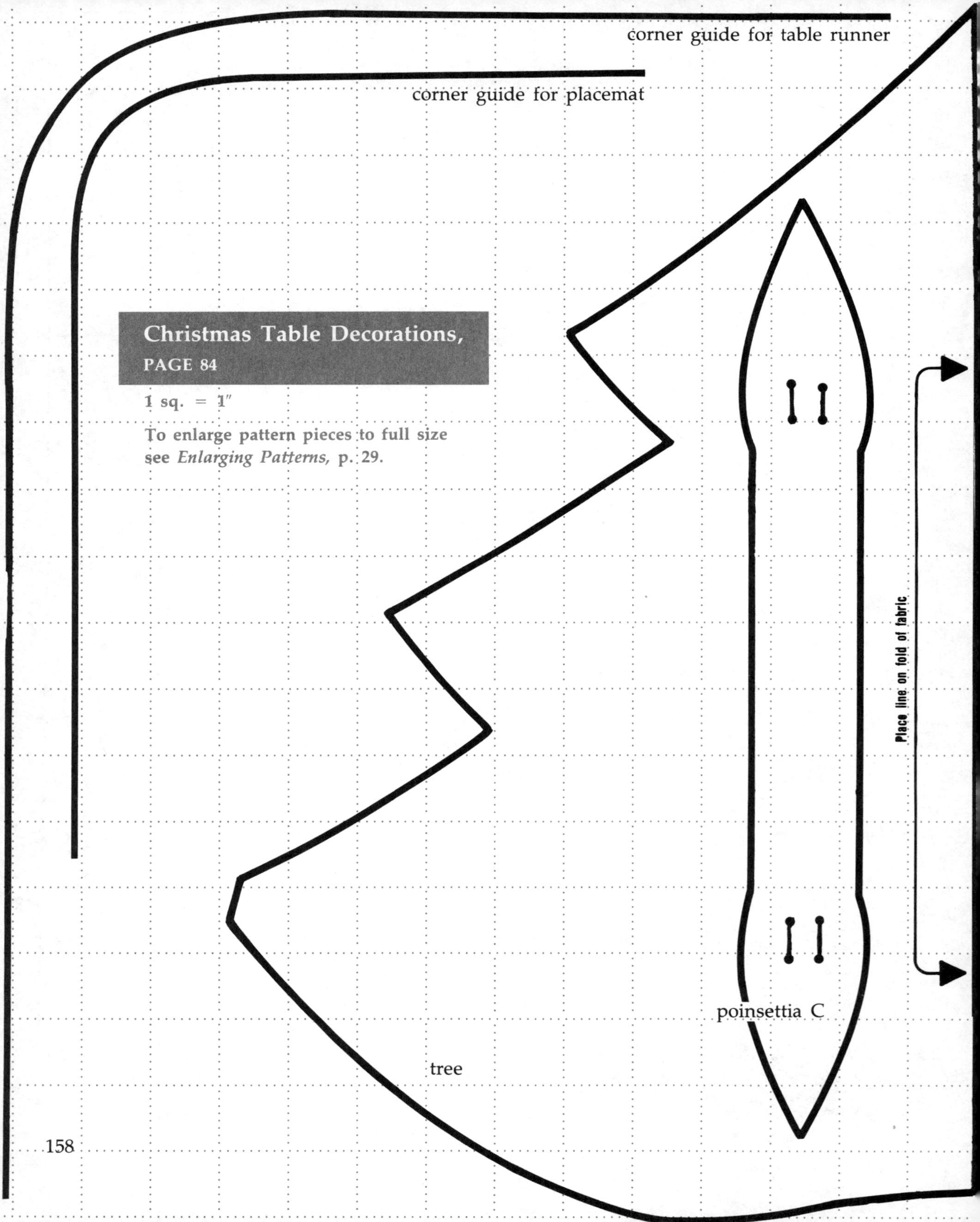

Place line on fold of fabric

poinsettia C

tree

158

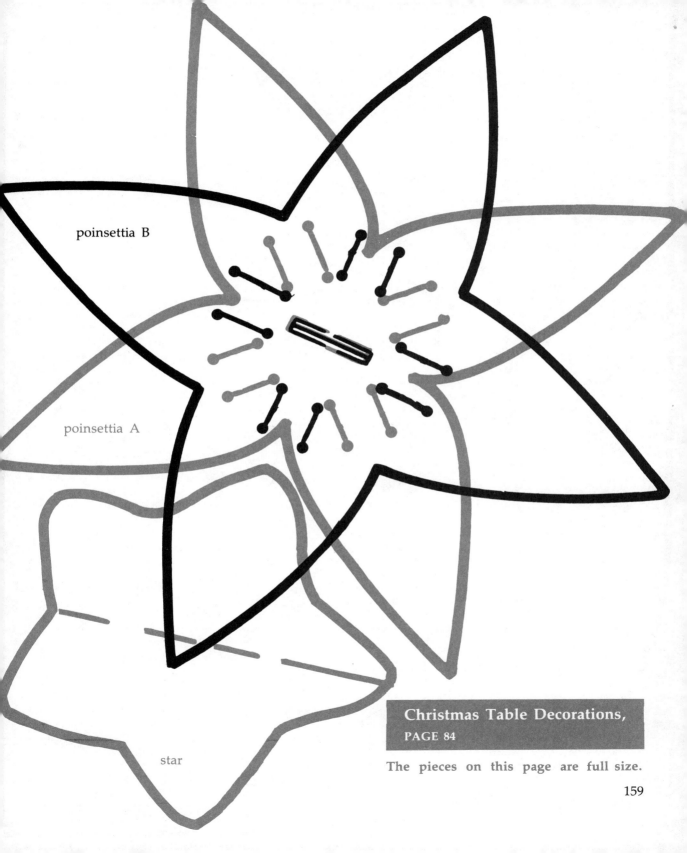

poinsettia B

poinsettia A

star

Christmas Table Decorations,
PAGE 84

The pieces on this page are full size.

159

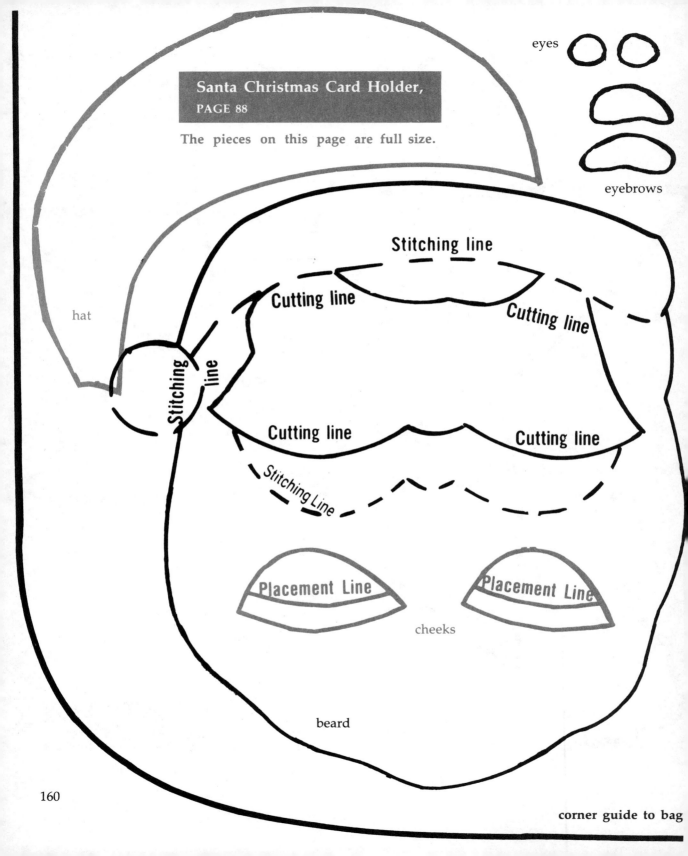

eyes

eyebrows

Santa Christmas Card Holder,
PAGE 88

The pieces on this page are full size.

hat

Stitching line

Cutting line

Stitching line

Cutting line

Stitching line

Cutting line

Cutting line

Stitching Line

Placement Line

Placement Line

cheeks

beard

160

corner guide to bag

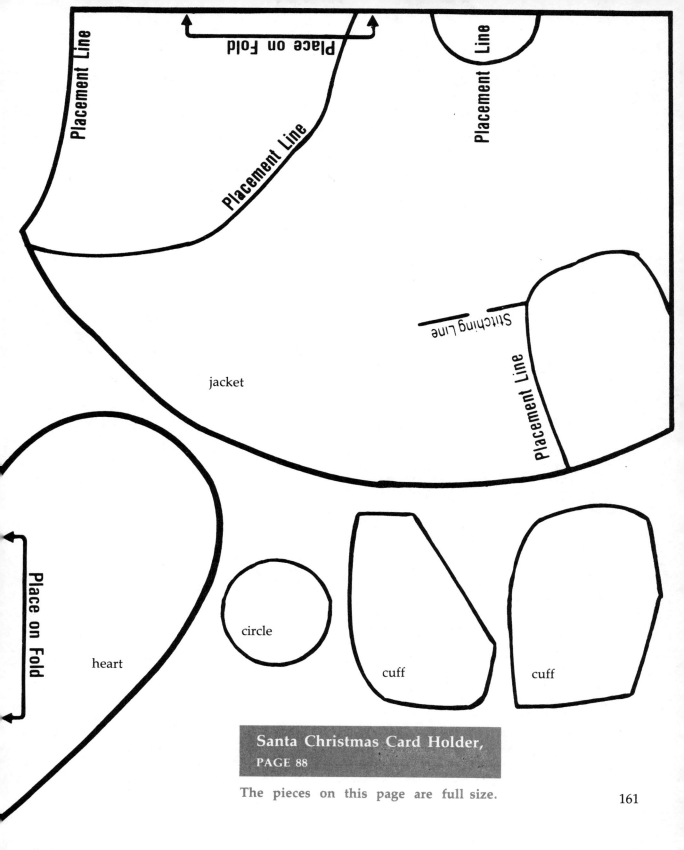

Placement Line

Place on Fold

Placement Line

Placement Line

jacket

Stitching Line

Placement Line

Place on Fold

heart

circle

cuff

cuff

The pieces on this page are full size.

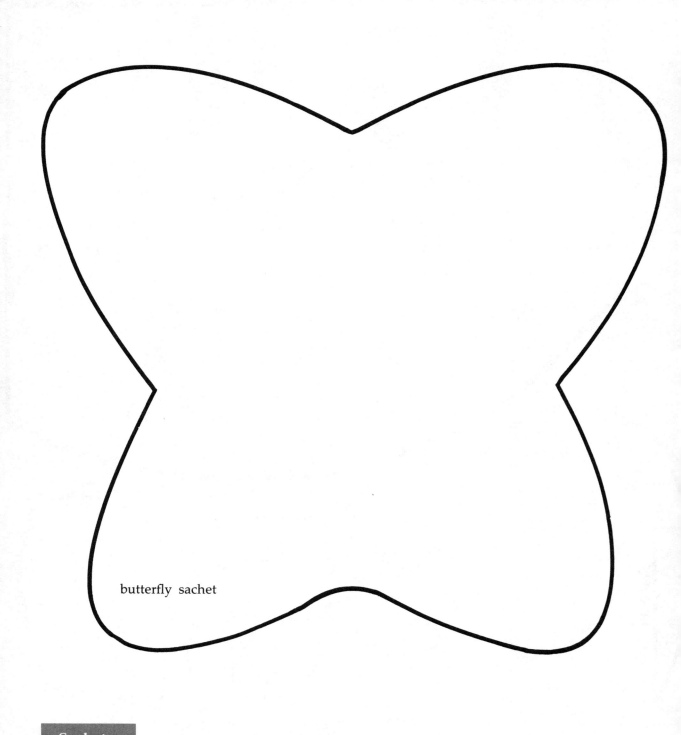

butterfly sachet

Sachets,
PAGE 92

The pieces on these pages are full size.

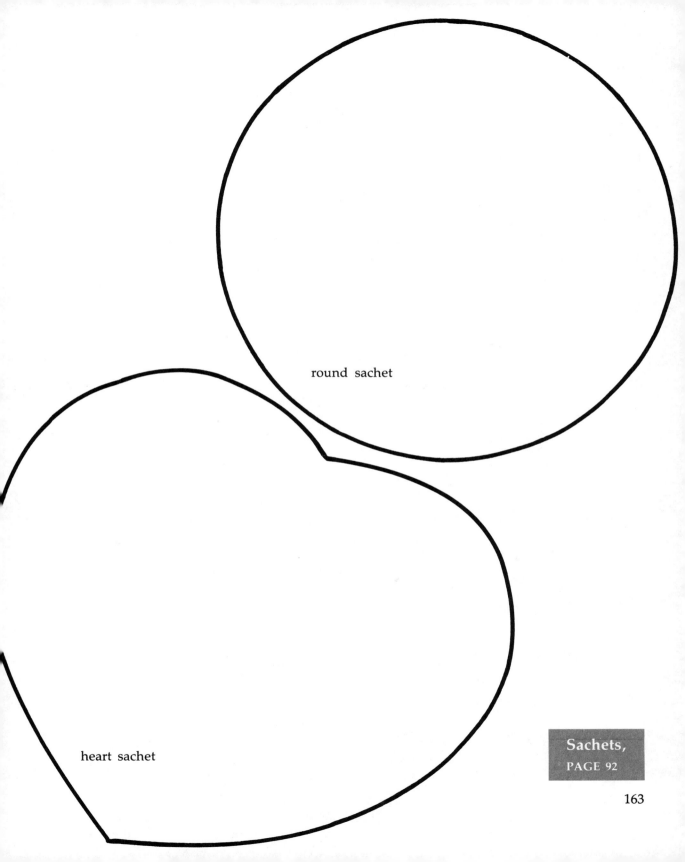

round sachet

heart sachet

Sachets,
PAGE 92

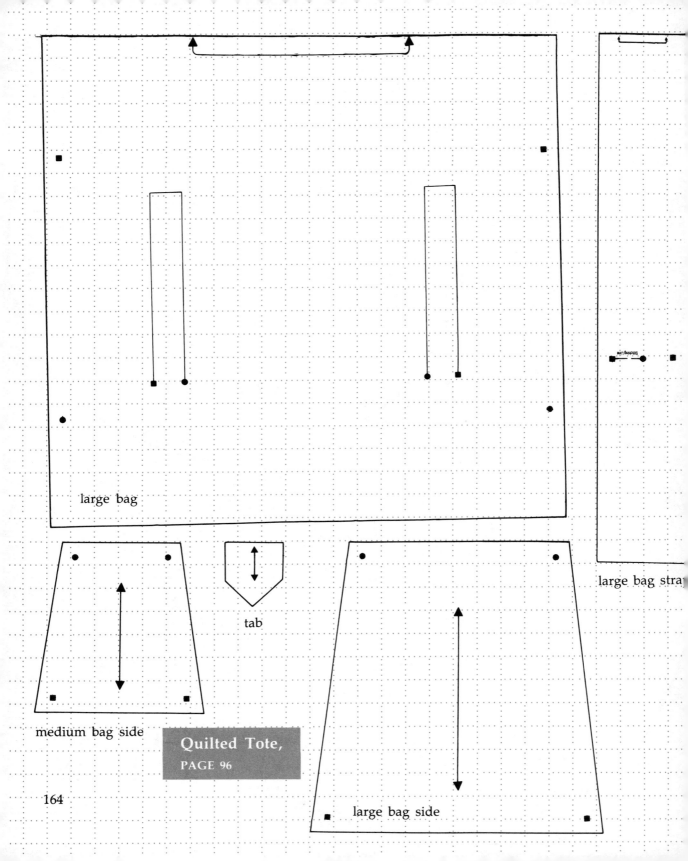

large bag

medium bag side

tab

large bag side

large bag stra

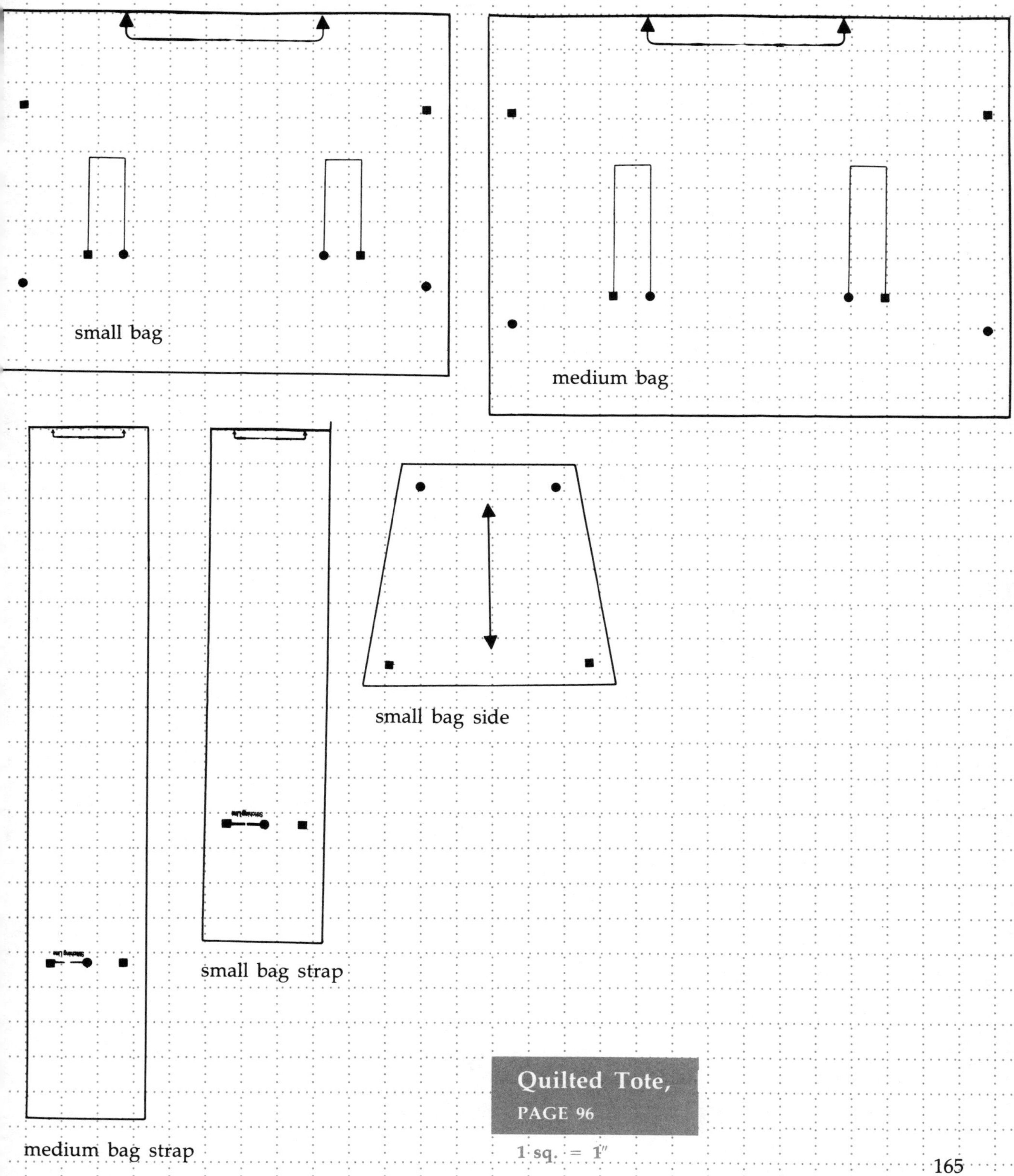

small bag

medium bag

small bag side

small bag strap

medium bag strap

Quilted Tote,
PAGE 96

1 sq. = 1"

To enlarge pattern pieces to full size
see *Enlarging Patterns*, p. 29.

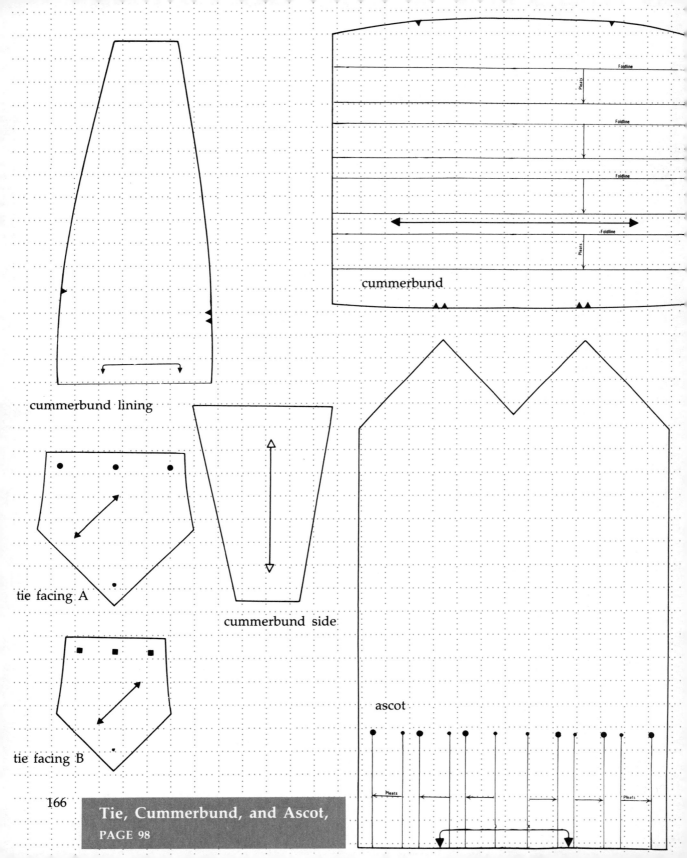

cummerbund

cummerbund lining

tie facing A

cummerbund side

tie facing B

ascot

Tie, Cummerbund, and Ascot,
PAGE 98

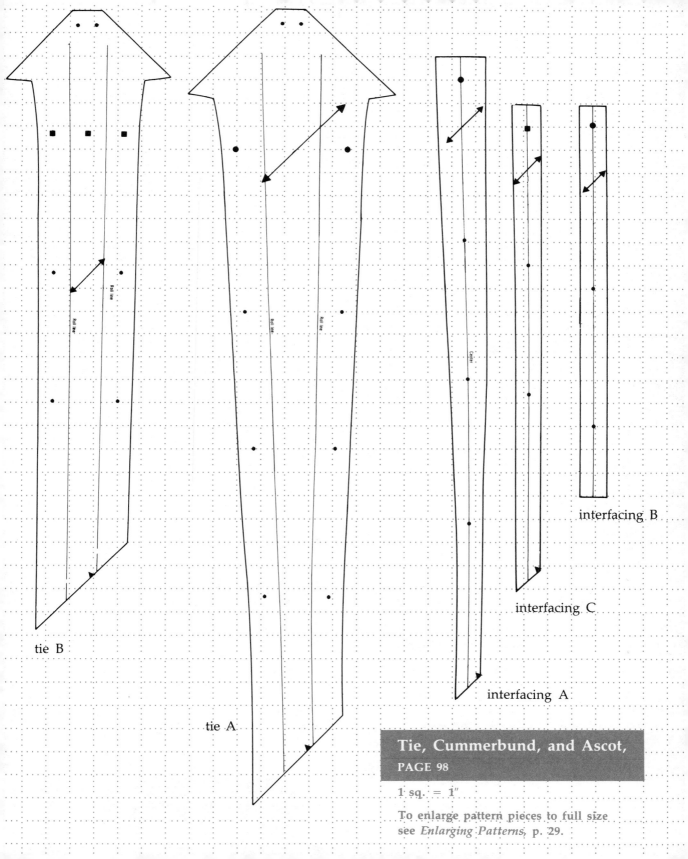

tie B

tie A

interfacing B

interfacing C

interfacing A

Tie, Cummerbund, and Ascot,
PAGE 98

1 sq. = 1″

To enlarge pattern pieces to full size
see *Enlarging Patterns*, p. 29.

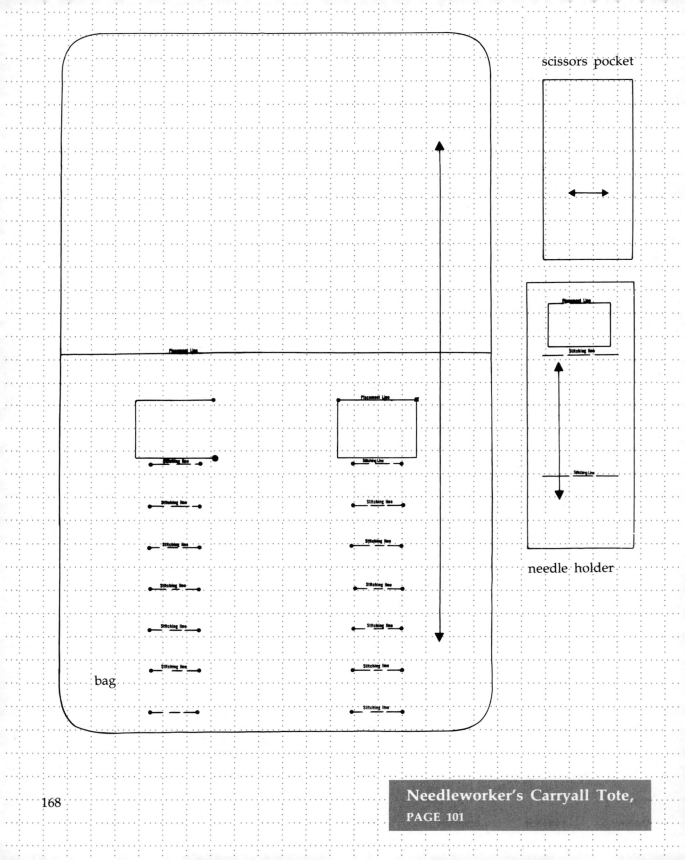

scissors pocket

needle holder

bag

Needleworker's Carryall Tote,
PAGE 101

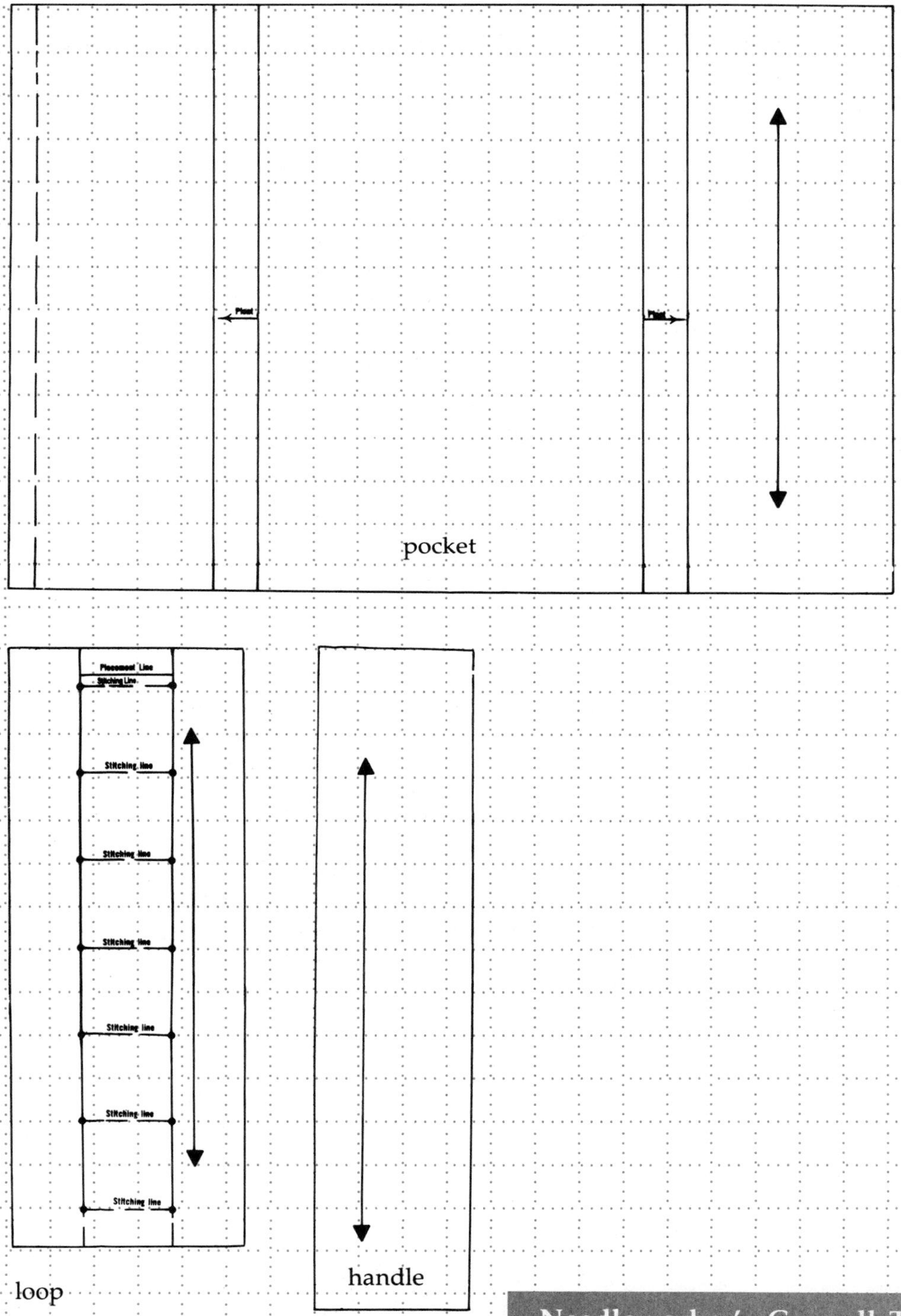

pocket

Placement Line
Stitching Line

Stitching line

Stitching line

Stitching line

Stitching line

Stitching line

Stitching line

loop

handle

1 sq. = 1"

169

To enlarge pattern pieces to full size
see *Enlarging Patterns*, p. 29.

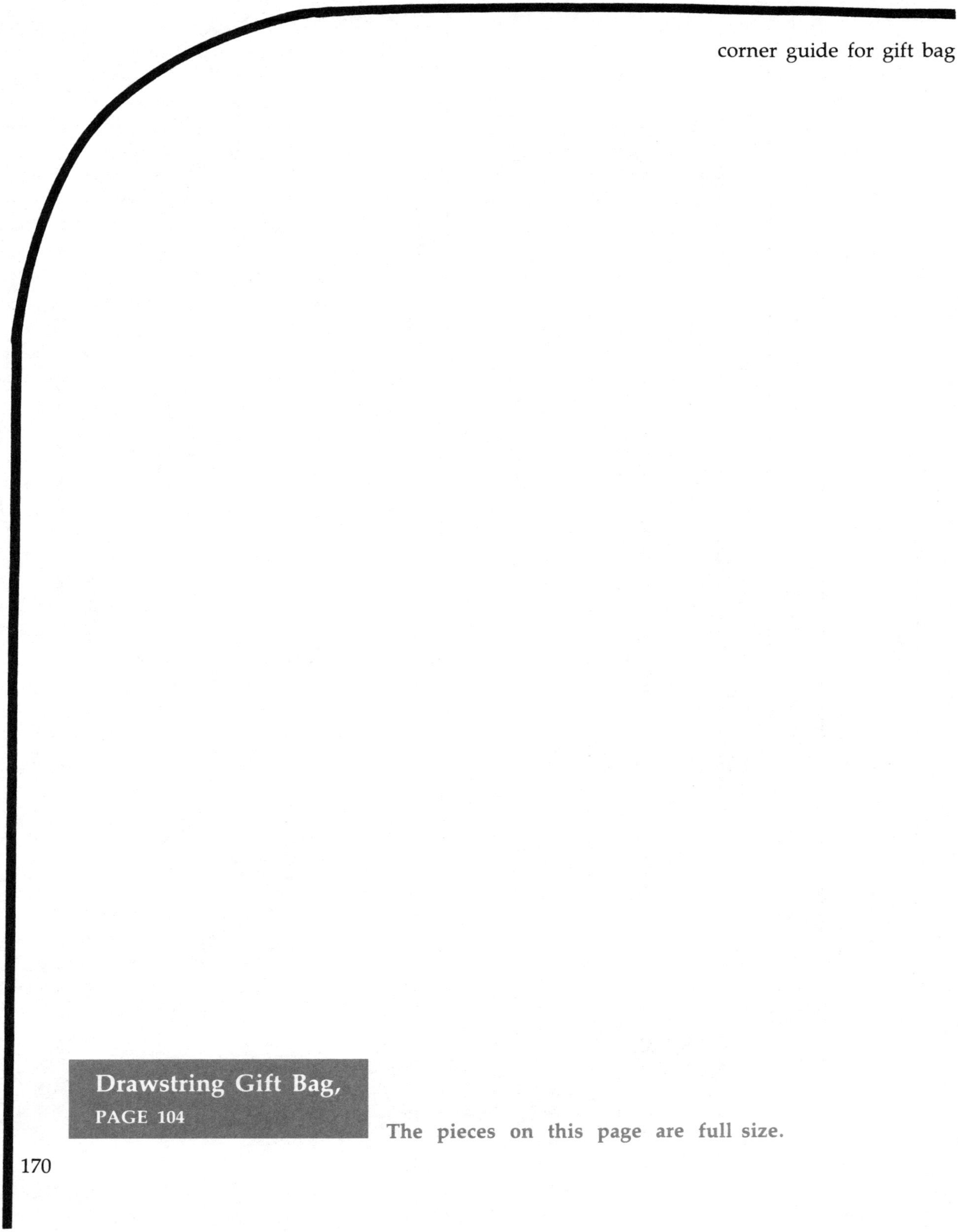

Drawstring Gift Bag,
PAGE 104

The pieces on this page are full size.

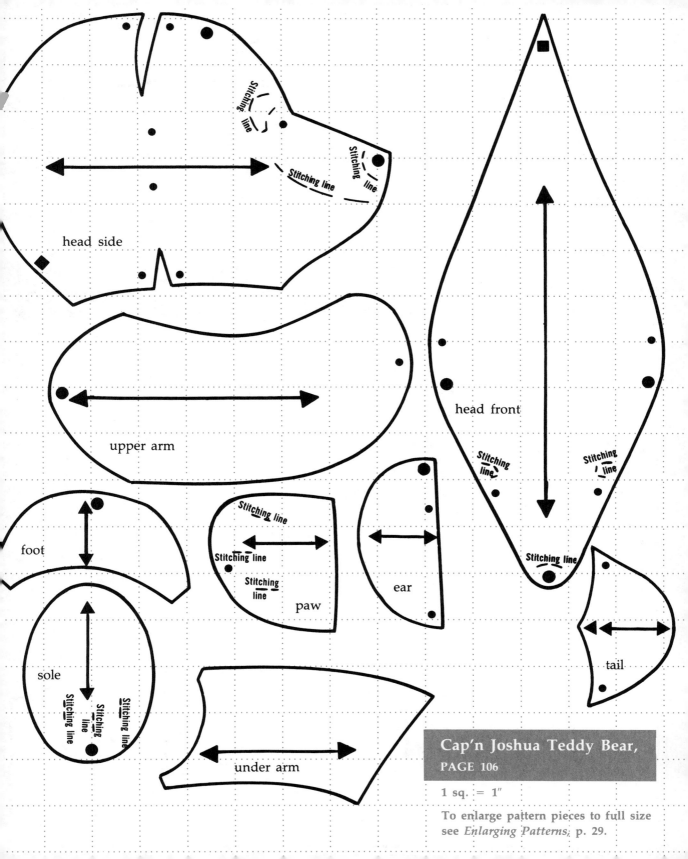

head side

Stitching line

Stitching line

Stitching line

upper arm

head front

Stitching line

Stitching line

Stitching line

foot

Stitching line

Stitching line

Stitching line

paw

ear

sole

Stitching line

Stitching line

Stitching line

under arm

tail

Cap'n Joshua Teddy Bear,
PAGE 106

1 sq. = 1″

To enlarge pattern pieces to full size
see *Enlarging Patterns*, p. 29.

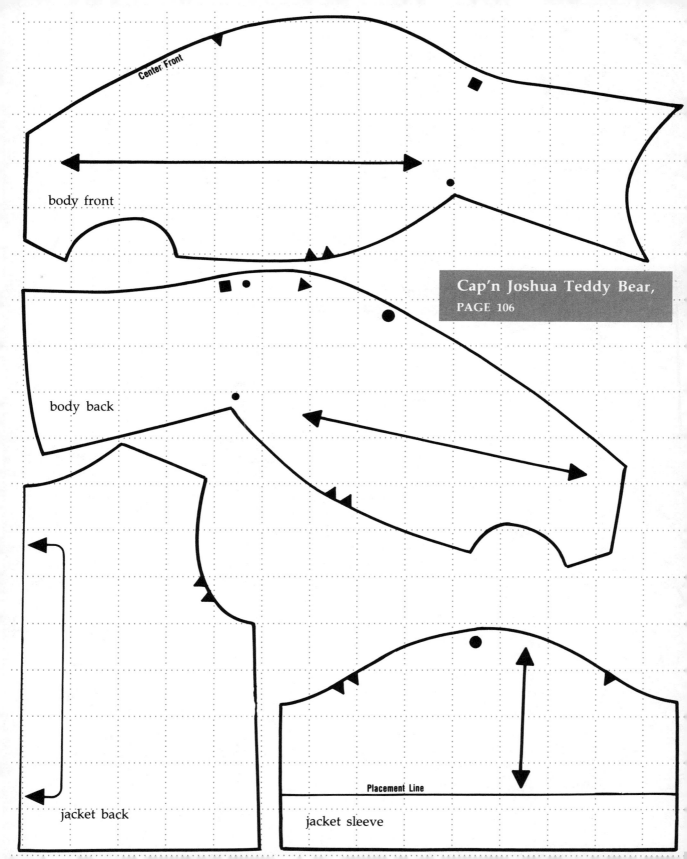

Center Front

body front

Cap'n Joshua Teddy Bear,
PAGE 106

body back

jacket back

Placement Line

jacket sleeve

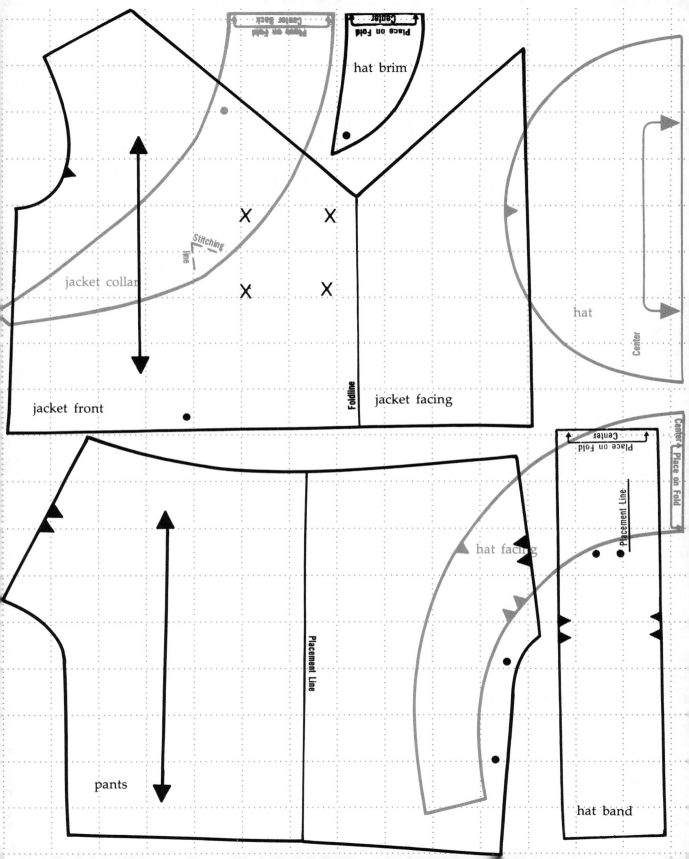

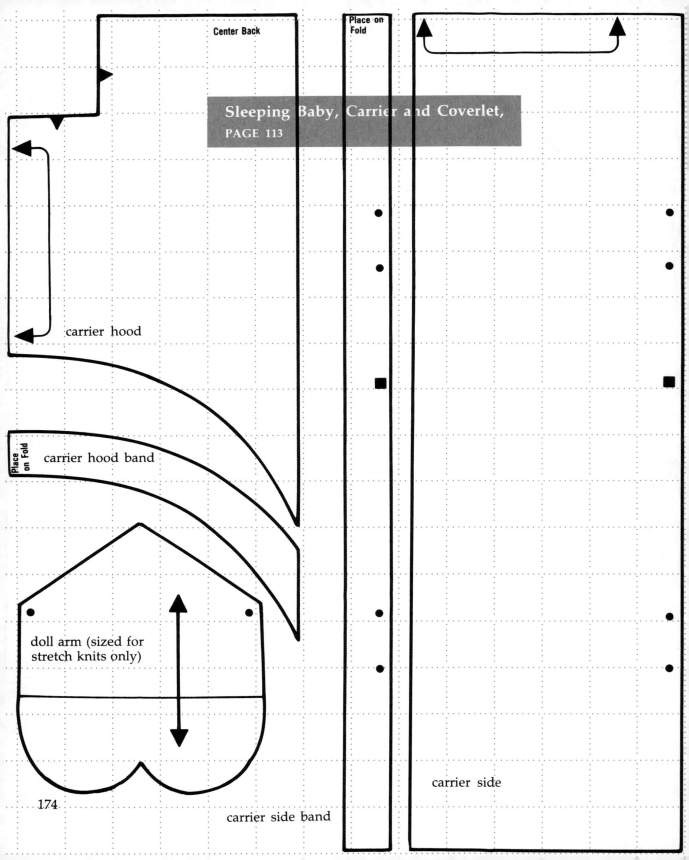

Center Back

Place on Fold

Sleeping Baby, Carrier and Coverlet,
PAGE 113

carrier hood

Place on Fold

carrier hood band

doll arm (sized for
stretch knits only)

174

carrier side

carrier side band

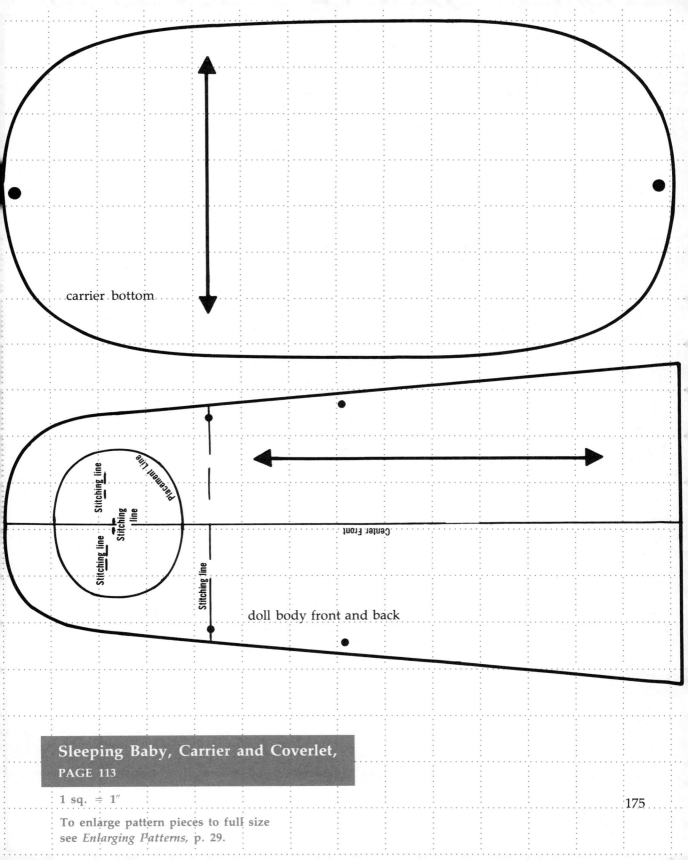

carrier bottom

Stitching line

Stitching line

Stitching line

Stitching line

Placement Line

Center Front

Stitching line

doll body front and back

Sleeping Baby, Carrier and Coverlet,
PAGE 113

1 sq. ≑ 1″

To enlarge pattern pieces to full size
see *Enlarging Patterns,* p. 29.

175

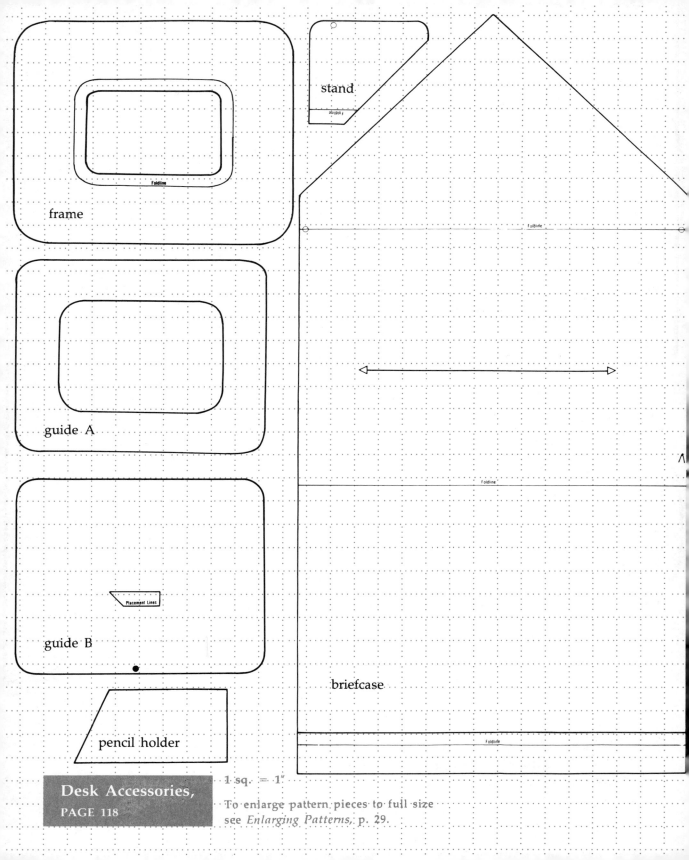

stand

frame

guide A

guide B

Placement Lines

pencil holder

briefcase

Foldline

Foldline

Foldline

Foldline

Foldline

1 sq. = 1"

To enlarge pattern pieces to full size
see *Enlarging Patterns,* p. 29.

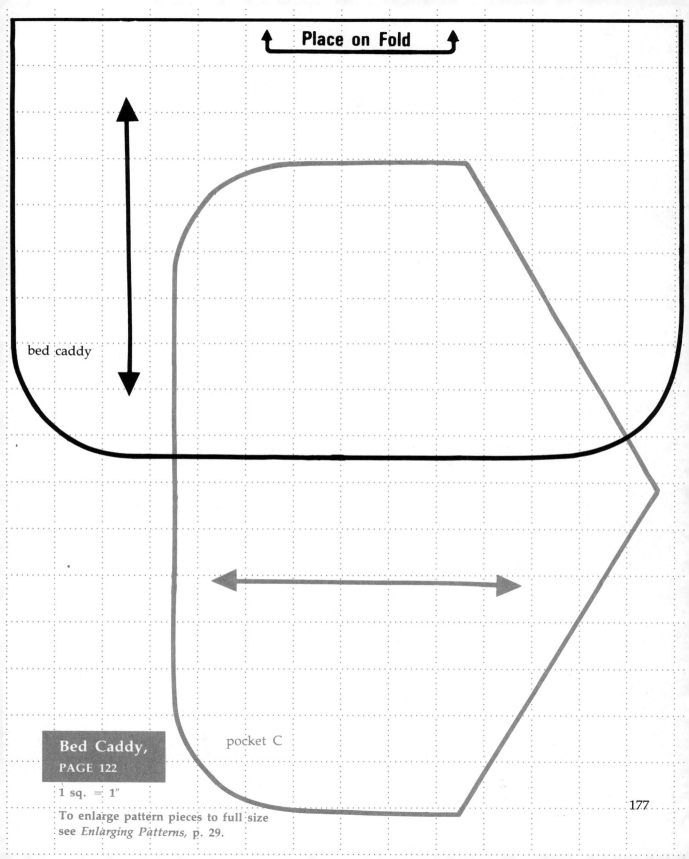

Place on Fold

bed caddy

Bed Caddy,
PAGE 122

1 sq. = 1"

To enlarge pattern pieces to full size
see *Enlarging Patterns,* p. 29.

pocket C

177

1 sq. = 1"

To enlarge pattern pieces to full size
see *Enlarging Patterns*, p. 29.

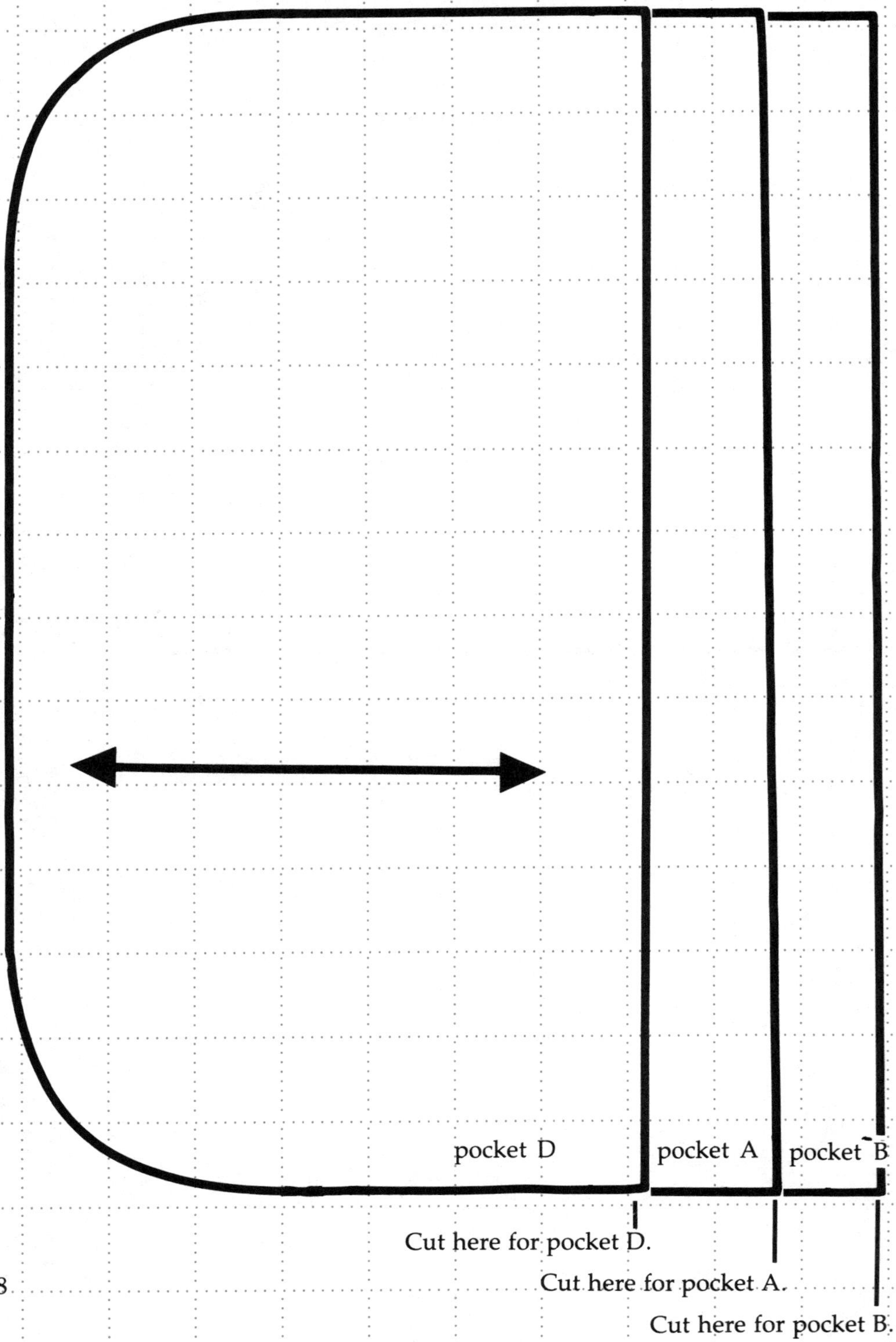

pocket D

pocket A

pocket B

Cut here for pocket D.

Cut here for pocket A.

Cut here for pocket B.

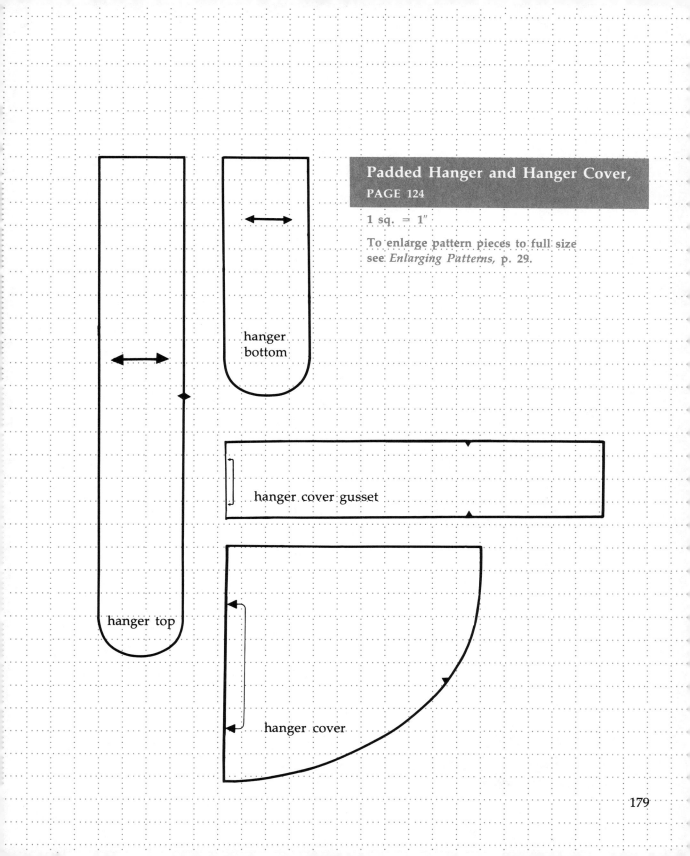

Padded Hanger and Hanger Cover,
PAGE 124

1 sq. = 1"

To enlarge pattern pieces to full size
see *Enlarging Patterns,* p. 29.

hanger
bottom

hanger cover gusset

hanger top

hanger cover

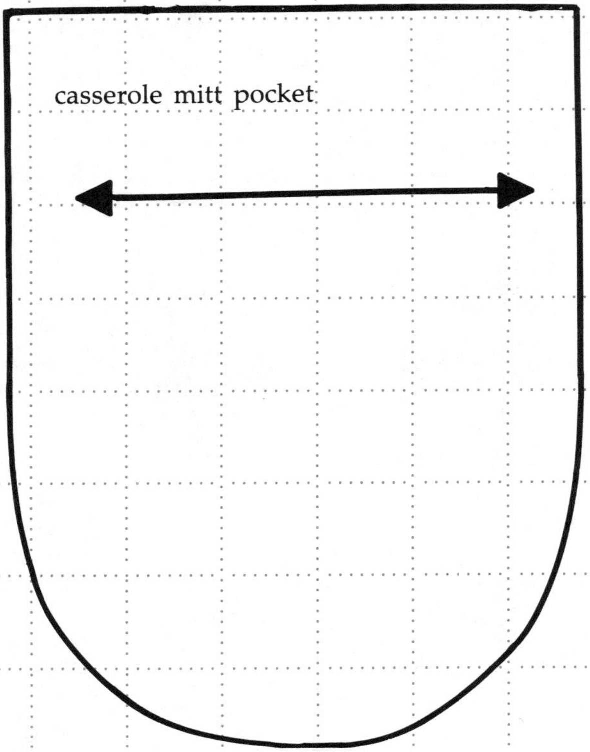

casserole mitt pocket

Place line on fold of fabric

Casserole and Oven Mitts,
PAGE 127

1 sq. = 1"

To enlarge pattern pieces to full size
see *Enlarging Patterns*, p. 29.

casserole mitt

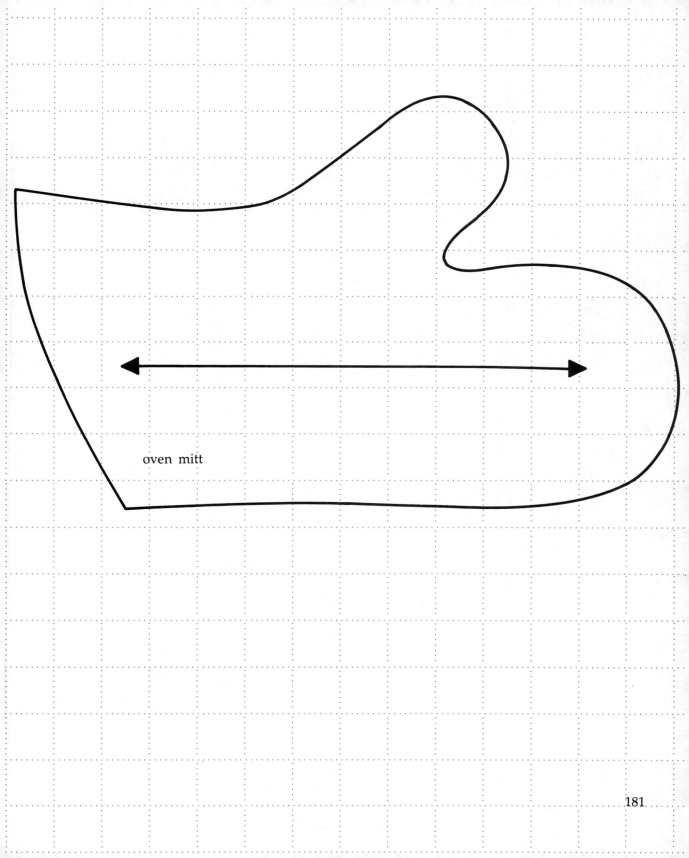

oven mitt

181

Monograms

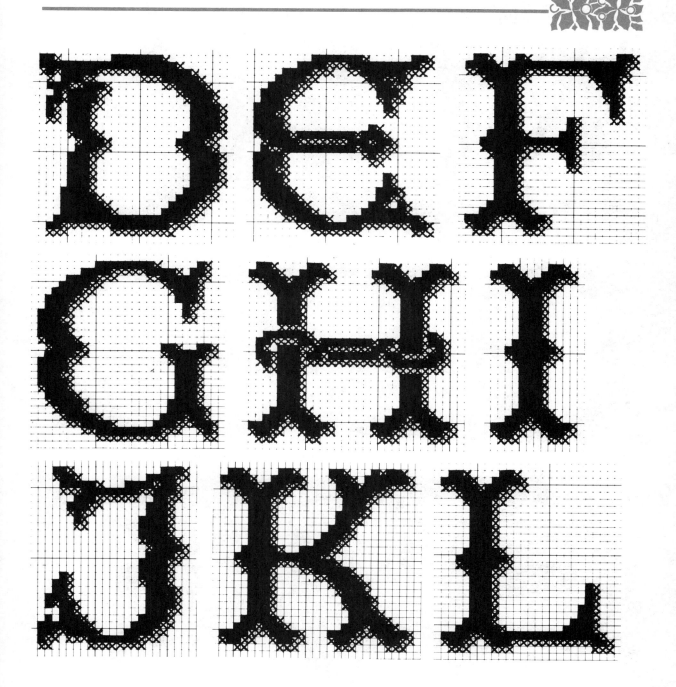

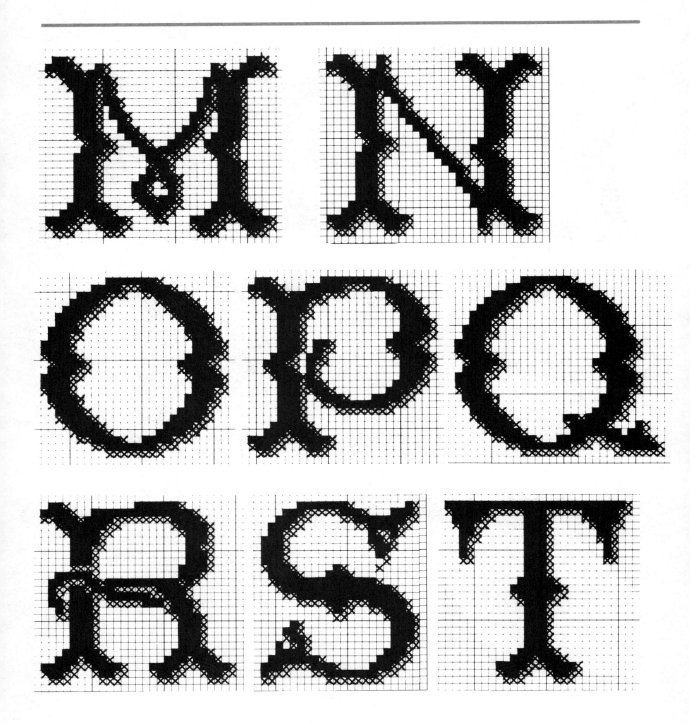

Index

191